The Post-Conciliar Church in Africa

african christian studies series (africs)

This series will make available significant works in the field of African Christian studies, taking into account the many forms of Christianity across the whole continent of Africa. African Christian studies is defined here as any scholarship that relates to themes and issues on the history, nature, identity, character, and place of African Christianity in world Christianity. It also refers to topics that address the continuing search for abundant life for Africans through multiple appeals to African religions and African Christianity in a challenging social context. The books in this series are expected to make significant contributions in historicizing trends in African Christian studies, while shifting the contemporary discourse in these areas from narrow theological concerns to a broader inter-disciplinary engagement with African religio-cultural traditions and Africa's challenging social context.

The series will cater to scholarly and educational texts in the areas of religious studies, theology, mission studies, biblical studies, philosophy, social justice, and other diverse issues current in African Christianity. We define these studies broadly and specifically as primarily focused on new voices, fresh perspectives, new approaches, and historical and cultural analyses that are emerging because of the significant place of African Christianity and African religio-cultural traditions in world Christianity. The series intends to continually fill a gap in African scholarship, especially in the areas of social analysis in African Christian studies, African philosophies, new biblical and narrative hermeneutical approaches to African theologies, and the challenges facing African women in today's Africa and within African Christianity. Other diverse themes in African Traditional Religions; African ecology; African ecclesiology; inter-cultural, inter-ethnic, and inter-religious dialogue; ecumenism; creative inculturation; African theologies of development, reconciliation, globalization, and poverty reduction will also be covered in this series.

SERIES EDITORS

Dr. Stan Chu Ilo (DePaul University, Chicago, USA)

Dr. Esther Acolatse (Duke University, Durham, USA)

Dr. Mwenda Ntarangwi (Calvin College, Grand Rapids, MI, USA)

The Post-Conciliar Church in Africa

No Turning Back the Clock

LAURENTI MAGESA

◈PICKWICK *Publications* · Eugene, Oregon

THE POST-CONCILIAR CHURCH IN AFRICA
No Turning Back the Clock

African Christian Studies Series

Copyright © 2018 Laurenti Magesa. All rights reserved. Except for brief quotations in critical publications or reviews, no part of this book may be reproduced in any manner without prior written permission from the publisher. Write: Permissions, Wipf and Stock Publishers, 199 W. 8th Ave., Suite 3, Eugene, OR 97401.

Pickwick Publications
An Imprint of Wipf and Stock Publishers
199 W. 8th Ave., Suite 3
Eugene, OR 97401

www.wipfandstock.com

PAPERBACK ISBN: 978-1-5326-0912-1
HARDCOVER ISBN: 978-1-5326-0914-5
EBOOK ISBN: 978-1-5326-0913-8

Cataloguing-in-Publication data:

Names: Magesa, Laurenti, 1946–, author.

Title: The post-conciliar church in Africa : no turning back the clock / Laurenti Magesa.

Description: Eugene, OR: Pickwick Publications, 2018 | Series: African Christian Studies Series | Includes bibliographical references.

Identifiers: ISBN 978-1-5326-0912-1 (paperback) | ISBN 978-1-5326-0914-5 (hardcover) | ISBN 978-1-5326-0913-8 (ebook)

Subjects: LCSH: Catholic Church—Africa | Catholic Church—Doctrines | Vatican Council (2nd : 1962–1965 : Basilica di San Pietro in Vaticano) | Conciliar theory

Classification: BX1751.3 M23 2018 (print) | BX1751.3 (ebook)

Manufactured in the U.S.A.   05/30/18

*I dedicate this book in a special way to my
teachers who showed me how:
Mr. Joseph B. Makongoro
(at Mabuimerafuru Primary School, Musoma, Tanzania);
Fr. Edward James, MM and Mr. Raphael Dibogo
(at Makoko Seminary, Musoma, Tanzania); and
Fr. Edward Wildsmith, MAfr
(at Nyegezi Seminary, Mwanza, Tanzania)*

*And to those who showed me why:
Fr. Lukas Malishi (at Ntungamo Seminary, Bukoba, Tanzania)
Fr. Norman Bevan, CSSp (at Kipalapala Seminary, Tabora, Tanzania)
Prof. Andre Guindon, OMI and Prof. Normand Provencher, OMI
(at St Paul University, Ottawa, Canada)*

*And to
Ms. Ndanu Mung'ala:
Tireless motivator*

Contents

Acknowledgements | ix
Prologue: Remarks by Pope Francis | xi
Introduction | xv

Chapter 1
Who Shaped Vatican II? | 1

Chapter 2
Tradition and Innovation at Vatican II | 5

Chapter 3
The Holy Spirit at Work | 10

Chapter 4
Collegial Leadership in the Church in Africa | 17

Chapter 5
Singing about God in an African Key | 21

Chapter 6
Culture as the Path of Faith | 26

Chapter 7
African Paths to Religious Life | 35

Chapter 8
Dialogue with African Religion | 46

Chapter 9
New Approaches to Mission | 59

CONTENTS

Chapter 10
The Public Role of the Church in Contemporary Africa | 71

Chapter 11
The Public Face of Theology | 84

Chapter 12
Models of Governance for Development in Africa | 95

Chapter 13
African Cultural Notions of Leadership | 108

Chapter 14
Violence, Justice, and Reconciliation | 115

Chapter 15
Human Sexuality in Africa | 123

Chapter 16
An African Reading of "Charity in Truth" | 130

Conclusion
No Turning Back the Clock | 141

Select Bibliography | 149

Acknowledgements

As PART OF ITS yearly "Winter Living Theology Programme," the Jesuit Institute of South Africa invited me to give a series of lectures in June 2012. I delivered the lectures in five cities across the country, namely in: Port Elizabeth, Cape Town, Durban, Bloemfontein, and Johannesburg. The lectures were attended by a wide range of people, including clergy, bishops, religious women and men, and laity. This volume is substantially based on the ideas presented in these lectures and the reactions they provoked.

I would like to thank Mr. Raymond Perrier, then organizer of the program at the Jesuit Institute, Johannesburg, for the initial invitation to deliver the lectures. I thank as well Dr. Anthony Egan, S.J. and Dr. Peter Knox, S.J. for their input in the planning and selecting of the theme for the lectures. The insights I received from all the participants in the five locations mentioned were invaluable. They stimulated me to further reflection and I have included many of their perceptions here.

My time in South Africa was both a wonderful experience and a moment of grace. Everywhere I went I received excellent hospitality and friendship from everyone, something I will continue to cherish. In this regard, I would like to single out in particular Fr. Chris Chatteris, S.J. in Cape Town and Dr. Gilbert Mardai, S.J. in Johannesburg for their care and concern.

In spite of my intention to compile these talks into a single publication early, it has taken me quite some time to do so on account of other academic engagements. A brief sabbatical offered to me by the Center for World Catholicism and Intercultural Theology, DePaul University in Chicago, USA, between January and May 2016, afforded me the perfect opportunity to actualize my intention. I am grateful to Prof. William Cavanaugh, Dr. Francis Salinel, Ms. Karen Kraft, and Prof. Stan Chu Ilo for facilitating the sabbatical. Many thanks too to the Vincentian Community at 2233 N. Kenmore Ave. where I resided for the duration of the sabbatical for the fraternal hospitality it provided me.

Itself an incomparable horizon in the life of the universal Church, Vatican II was a landmark that deliberately intended to point to further horizons. In a figure of speech, we can appropriately describe the Council as an inexhaustible goldmine that is always open for further exploration and discovery. Pope Francis frequently and in various ways reminds us of this fact. I publish these reflections to celebrate fifty years of Vatican II and the hope it represents for the future of the Church in Africa. I offer them as a stimulus for African (Catholic) Christians to continue digging deeper into and benefitting from the spiritual treasure that the Council still holds forth for us for a long time to come.

For the theologian or historian of Vatican II, some of the preliminary information in this volume may be quite familiar, even elementary. Yet all of it is important if one is to grasp the scope, meaning and implications of the Council for the Church and people of Africa.

Because the book is a result of oral presentations and is intended also for the non-academic readership, I have avoided a lot of academic details which would unnecessarily distract from the flow of the book. Thus, although I have tried to acknowledge my sources, I have deliberately dispensed from unnecessary footnotes except where I thought it absolutely necessary for the reader to consult further for more insights. The bibliography at the end of the book provides many of the sources for my information.

Laurenti Magesa

Prologue

Remarks by Pope Francis

On the Relationship between the Churches

The young Catholic Churches, as they grow, develop a synthesis of faith, culture, and life, and so it is a synthesis different from the one developed by the ancient Churches. ... [T]he relationship between the ancient Catholic Churches and the young ones is similar to the relationship between young and elderly people in a society. They build the future, the young ones with their strength and the others with their wisdom. You always run some risks, of course. The younger Churches are likely to feel self-sufficient; the ancient ones are likely to want to impose on the younger Churches their cultural models. But we build the future together.

INTERVIEW WITH FR. ANTONIO SPADARO, S.J.
"A BIG HEART OPEN TO GOD."

REMARKS BY POPE FRANCIS

On Vatican II

Vatican II was a re-reading of the Gospel in the light of contemporary culture. . . . Vatican II produced a renewal movement that simply comes from the same Gospel. Its fruits are enormous. Just recall the liturgy. The work of liturgical reform has been a service to the people as a re-reading of the Gospel from a concrete historical situation. Yes, there are hermeneutics of continuity and discontinuity, but one thing is clear: the dynamic of reading the Gospel, actualizing its message for today—which was typical of Vatican II—is absolutely irreversible.

INTERVIEW WITH FR. ANTONIO SPADARO, S.J.
"A BIG HEART OPEN TO GOD."

On Methods of Evangelization

When properly understood, cultural diversity is not a threat to Church unity. The Holy Spirit, sent by the Father and the Son, transforms our hearts and enables us to enter into the perfect communion of the blessed Trinity, where all things find their unity. He builds up the communion and harmony of the people of God. The same Spirit is that harmony, just as he is the bond of love between the Father and the Son. It is he who brings forth a rich variety of gifts, while at the same time creating a unity which is never uniformity but a multifaceted and inviting harmony. Evangelization joyfully acknowledges these varied treasures which the Holy Spirit pours out upon the Church. We would not do justice to the logic of the Incarnation if we thought of Christianity as monocultural and monotonous. While it is true that some cultures have been closely associated with the preaching of the Gospel and the development of Christian thought, the revealed message is not identified with any of them; its content is transcultural. Hence in the evangelization of new cultures, or cultures which have not received the Christian message, it is not essential to impose a specific cultural form, no matter how beautiful or ancient it may be, together with the Gospel. The message that we proclaim always has a certain cultural dress, but we in the Church can sometimes fall into a needless hallowing of our own culture, and thus show more fanaticism than true evangelizing zeal....

We cannot demand that peoples of every continent, in expressing their Christian faith, imitate modes of expression which European nations developed at a particular moment of their history, because the faith cannot be constricted to the limits of understanding and expression of any one culture. It is an indisputable fact that no single culture can exhaust the mystery of our redemption in Christ.

EVANGELII GAUDIUM, 118–19

Introduction

EACH OF THE TWENTY Ecumenical Councils of the Catholic Church before the Second Vatican Council (Vatican II, 1962–65) can be described accurately as an end of a process. Each one of them was called to refute an error in the teaching or the practice of the faith. As a consequence, each established a precise doctrinal position, or a particular disciplinary pronouncement.

Some of the most important and enduring doctrines formulated by these Councils included the Divinity of Christ (defined by Nicaea I in 325 followed by Constantinople I in 381); the Divine Motherhood of Mary (Ephesus, 431); and the Distinct Human and Divine Natures in Christ (Chalcedon, 451). Other doctrines and practices the Councils defined concerned the appropriateness of the veneration of icons and images in the liturgy (Nicaea II, 787); the Election of a Pope by a two-thirds majority of cardinals (Lateran III, 1179); the Eucharistic Doctrine of Transubstantiation, and the requirement that Catholics go to confession at least once a year (Lateran IV, 1215). Defined as well were: the teaching on the Holy Spirit as proceeding "from the Father and the Son" (Lyons II, 1274); the composition of the teaching authority of the Church, the nature of original sin, the sacraments, and structure of the formation of the clergy (Trent, 1545–63). Vatican I (1869–70), the Twentieth Ecumenical Council, established as Catholic teaching, the primacy and infallibility of the Pope and condemned both rationalism and fideism.

Though maintaining the essential internal faith of the Church, as well as doctrinal and practical continuity with all the previous Councils, the Twenty-first Council, the Second Vatican Council (Vatican II, 1962–65), was distinctly different from the others in one most significant aspect. In all the areas it discussed, this Council did not see itself as an end of a process but, actually, as a beginning. It opened, not closed, doors, whether doctrinal or disciplinary for ongoing reflection, for possibilities of ever-improved knowledge and understanding. This was what Pope John XXIII, the Council's architect, referred to as *aggiornamento*, the openness of the faith and the mission of the Church to the world. The pried Church doors, for so long closed, to embrace the world and cooperate with it with the goal of bringing it to God. Again, this process was described as *rapprochement*, continuous encounter with, not paranoid flight from, the world. The principles having been laid down by the Council, the question for the subsequent generations was how practically to achieve them.

Fifty years on today after the close of the Council, the question, and therefore the process, is still open—perhaps even more so than the Council Fathers themselves imagined. More than at any other period in human history, the world is changing faster and faster. In the last fifty years alone, changes have taken place in science, medicine, and information and communications technology—and therefore in politics, economics, and human relations—that could hardly have been thought possible prior in the 1960s when Vatican II was taking place. These changes bring with them live challenges to the principles established by the Council, but in the spirit of these principles, the challenges we now encounter invite all Catholics to continue the dialogue with the world, to open new avenues of understanding of the divine plan in the universe, and to try to see further horizons of the faith of the Church. What this means is that the principles launched by Vatican II are as alive and open today as they were fifty odd years ago.

Vatican II can therefore be understood correctly as a "source of living water," in the sense that we can go to the Council again and again to try to understand the meaning of the Catholic faith in the world. In this sense it is like the Gospels. Its springs must never be blocked but must remain open to nourish the faithful and quench the ever-present human thirst for God. Perhaps Vatican II will lead to Vatican III, or Nairobi I, or Dar es Salaam I, or Mumbai I in the near or distant future. However, any one of these, whenever they happen, will be an offspring of Vatican II as continuation of the process initiated there, and will in no way imply a termination of it. For the particular gift of Vatican II, in distinction from the previous Councils, was the unambiguous realization that the aggiornamento and the rapprochement the Church as a faith community seeks is a never-ending affair. It is a lasting encounter of love between humanity, the universe, and God.

For the vitality of the Gospel of Christ in the life of the Church throughout the world—and in our particular case, in Africa—we must return again and again to the Council, to its origins, development, insights, and horizons.

We must revisit its spirit, its promises, and achievements. We must evaluate sincerely and in fidelity to the Church, the shortcomings in its implementation so far, in order to go forward. No one succeeds who has not failed at one time or another. As the anonymous poet rightly put it, "Success is failure turned inside out." As the Council event goes beyond its fiftieth year, it is a hallowed moment for our own specific African location to keep up the tempo of reflection in celebration of the gift to the Church that was Vatican II.

Chapter 1

Who Shaped Vatican II?

THE OBVIOUS QUESTION TO ask about Vatican II and the Church in Africa is this: was the African theological and pastoral view present at the Council? The answer is quite frankly, not really! At the first seven Ecumenical Councils of the Church (namely: Nicaea I, Constantinople I, Ephesus, Chalcedon, Constantinople II, Constantinople III, and Nicaea II), Africa's voice was very much present. The Church then was still strong in the northern regions of Africa before the Muslim invasion and conquest there in the seventh century. So Africa, or, more precisely, that part of northern Africa that had received the Gospel then, was generally fairly well represented in these Councils—if, perhaps, not in numbers, at least in political diplomacy and theological muscle. One notes in this respect the theological acumen and leadership authority of The Episcopal Sees of Alexandria and Carthage in these early meetings. With Vatican II, however, the story is different.

Statistics and percentages will help to draw the picture.[1] Of the approximately 2,860 fathers who attended the four sessions of the Council, only about 10 percent, or a total of about three hundred bishops, came from Africa. Of these only about thirty were indigenous. The rest belonged to missionary organizations. This means that they predominantly represented the theological and pastoral views of their European-sending Institutes. But one wonders whether even the indigenous African bishops at the Council could have been expected to reflect African theological and pastoral standpoints. Though reportedly remarkably well organized, on account of their small number and

---

1. For most of what follows, see O'Malley, *What Happened at Vatican II*, 2008.

lack of Africa-oriented theological expertise, their theological and pastoral views were easily overshadowed. Unlike their counterparts from Europe, African bishops did not as yet have qualified theological experts (*periti*) to advise them. Moreover, they all had been trained in the Roman or Latin Catholic academic philosophical and theological traditions and inevitably mirrored this training in their thinking and contributions.

Bishops Joseph Blomjous of Mwanza, Tanzania, Vincent McCauley of Fort Portal, Uganda, Marcel Lefebvre of Dakar, Senegal, and Denis Hurley of Durban, South Africa, were the "stars" from Africa. But all of them were missionaries, belonging to European Mission Institutes. Among the indigenous or native-born and diocesan-priest bishops, there were Laurean Rugambwa of Bukoba, Tanzania, and Joseph Albert Malula of the then Leopoldville, Zaire (now Kinshasa, DRC). Again, it is true that whatever interventions the latter made on the Council floor were highly influenced by their missionary colleagues. For this reason, some Church historians have claimed, rather implausibly, that the missionary bishops must have ghostwritten these interventions for them. Whatever the case may be about this issue, it is certain that African voices did not impact very much the deliberations and outcome of the Council, not least because the Council was palpably Eurocentric in its structure and agenda.

Though largely muffled and unable to influence the general orientation of the Council, a few voices from Africa were nevertheless incisive. One was Bishop Soares de Resende of Beira in Mozambique, who even then wanted a Church of and for the poor, questioning the value of ornate Church decoration and insignia as not being in accordance with the Spirit of Christ. Another was Bishop Raymond Tchidimbo of Conakry in Guinea. He complained about the "Western outlook" of sections of the schema on the Church in the world today. As he saw it, the draft did not pay enough attention to the difficulties the people of Africa were suffering under the yoke of "poverty," "underdevelopment," "colonialism," and "discrimination." It is somewhat surprising that the noted anti-apartheid campaigner Bishop Hurley is not recorded to have condemned this aberration against human dignity and rights in his official submissions.

The driving engine of the Council was understandably made up mainly of European and North American cardinals, archbishops, and bishops, and their expert theologians. A list of the most significant prelates at the Council must include names like the Archbishop of Milan, Giovanni Battista Montini (later to become Pope Paul VI), the Archbishop of Krakow, Karol Wojtyla (later to become Pope John Paul II), and Professor Joseph Ratzinger (later to become Pope Benedict XVI). Other significant personalities were Cardinals Jan Bernard Alfrink from the Netherlands, Leon-Joseph Suenens from Belgium, Augustin Bea, Joseph Frings and Julius Dopfner from Germany, Franz Konig from Austria, and Eugene Tisserant and Giuseppe Siri from France and Italy respectively. From North America, most notable were Cardinal Francis Spellman of New York, Cardinal Albert Meyer of Chicago, Archbishop John E. Dearden of Detroit, and Cardinal James Francis McIntyre of Los Angeles, U.S.A. Another powerful voice was in the person of Cardinal Paul-Emile Leger of Montreal, Canada.

The experts who swayed the course of the Council were again, understandably, predominantly European theologians. Several of them had been suspect in Rome for their theological views before the Council and some had even been ostracized to different degrees by the Vatican authorities. But because of their work during the Council, they became household names in seminaries and theological institutes everywhere afterwards. They included MarieDominique Chenu, OP, Yves-Marie Congar, OP, Jean Danielou, SJ, Henri de Lubac, SJ, and the layman philosopher Jacques Maritain, all French nationals. Others were the Dutchman Edward Schillebeeckx, OP, the German Karl Rahner, SJ, and Bernard Haring, CSSR. From America there was John Courtney Murray, SJ. Given the fact that Vatican II took place at a time when the push to recognize African identity through the struggle for independence was going on in the political sphere, it is odd again that no theologian from Africa appears on this list as advisor to an African bishop even though there was already a sizeable number of educated African clergy at this time. The collection of essays under the title *Des pretres noirs s'interrogent* by African priests studying in France had already been published in 1956, six years before the opening of the Council. Thus, the failure of the bishops from Africa to employ the continent's theologians' input at the Council is strange.

However, the presence of an African lay auditor at the Council, Eusebe Adjakpley from Togo, though not well known, was "symbolic." Adjakpley was regional secretary for Africa of the International Federation of Catholic Youth. One of around forty lay and religious observers at the Council during its third and fourth sessions, he made an important intervention on mission. Unfortunately, in subsequent years, the possibility of building up an ecclesiology of communion and *sensus fidelium* in the Church in Africa, reflecting the role of the laity in the Church as was provided by the presence of Adjakpley and his fellow auditors, was not immediately taken up in any sustained way by the Church in Africa, even in the wake of the Decree on the Apostolate of the Laity, *Apostolicam Actuositatem* of 1965. It would not be until almost a decade later, in the 1970s, that the hierarchy in some parts of the continent would establish the largely lay-organized pastoral plan and structure of Small Christian Communities as a "pastoral priority" for the Church.

Was, therefore, Vatican II completely lost on Africa? To put the same question in other words, in spite of the insignificant contribution of the Church in Africa at Vatican II as an event, how significant, if at all, has the Council been as a factor in the development of the Church in Africa during the intervening five decades? Part of the answer lies in the dynamics of the Council-event itself. Despite the precise planning and some attempts at stage-management, once begun, the Council took its own course some of whose consequences were unexpected and, in diverse ways, affected the Church in every part of the world.

Chapter 2

Tradition and Innovation at Vatican II

"Whatever you are, be a good one!"

THIS WITTICISM, ATTRIBUTED TO Abraham Lincoln, describes accurately what happened at Vatican II. From the announcement of the intention to convene it by Pope John XXIII on January 25, 1959 to its conclusion on December 8, 1965 under Pope Paul VI, its four sessions, each lasting for about ten weeks, were meticulously planned and the discussions relatively well executed. As with every meeting, but especially with one of such size and diversity, there were some organizational and procedural hitches here and there. But these were minor compared to what the Council was finally able to achieve theologically as well as pastorally. Thus, as a Council, Vatican II, whatever else it was, was a good one.

The history of the Council, from its preparation and actual floor discussions until the promulgation of the final sixteen documents, fills volumes. It has been characterized by notable historians of Christianity as "a remarkable Council," distinguishing itself in every way from any other in history by its size, composition, and variety of topics discussed (its agenda). It still may be ranked as perhaps the biggest and longest meeting in the history of the Church. With about two thousand bishop delegates attending any one of the four sessions, nearly 480 theological advisors, and many observers, this claim is easily borne out. The documentation of discussion at the Council runs into approximately thirty thousand pages, nearly a third of all previous recognized Ecumenical Councils. The media, initially sluggish in reporting the Conciliar proceedings, finally caught up with the importance of this meeting. Now many people around the world could read about the events about the Council in newspapers, listen over the radio, or watch on television from their homes.

By the mid-twentieth century, Catholic missionary work had spread and established itself in most parts of the world. In Africa, through conditions made possible by colonialism, Christianity in general, and the Catholic Church in particular, had dioceses and mission stations throughout the continent. As mentioned, expatriate missionaries were still manning most of these dioceses and mission stations as bishops and priests. But there were now increasing numbers of local men being ordained as priests and religious. Among them a few began to be consecrated bishops. Although seminary philosophical and theological training was uniform worldwide, drawing from the paradigm established earlier by the Council of Trent, the cultural expressions of this training could not be completely obliterated among these African Church leaders. Though the Conciliar deliberations were predominantly of European and North American preferences, as we have indicated in the preceding chapter, their interpretation by African bishops back home was not completely devoid of an African flavor.

The drafts of each one of the Conciliar documents went through rigorous scrutiny. Here, let us merely draw a portrait of how the Council navigated through two equally important pulls: one of tradition and the other of innovation. Both were palpable among the prelates and theologians at the Council. At the end of the day and going by the documents adopted, did the Council manage to balance these two forces and if so, how?

In The Bull, *Humani Salutis* of December 25, 1961, which formally instituted the Council, Pope John XXIII had already articulated the tension between the old and the new in terms of the relationship between the world of science and the faith of the Church inspired by the Gospel of Christ. This was to form the major test for the Council because this was its social context. Pope John XXIII had noted that "In the face of this twofold spectacle—a world that displays a serious state of spiritual poverty and the Church of Christ, still so vibrant with vitality," the purpose of the Council was "to give the Church the possibility to contribute more effectively to the solutions of the problems of the modern age."[1] In the Council, some thought that they had to choose between *rapprochement* or *aggiornamento* and safeguarding "Church teaching." But Pope John XXIII's intention was to preserve a healthy tension between both to give birth to a new Church open to the world where, spiritually, both would win.

Therefore, in spite of various cultural, philosophical, and theological outlooks of the bishops, and the traditional or liberal-conservative mood

1. See "Pope John XXIII Convokes"

crisscrossing the conversations, what underlay the Council's discussions, and the documents that emerged, was how the faith perennially expressed in traditional teaching of the Church could be brought to address modern human concerns and needs. Pope John XXIII explained this goal before the beginning of the Council in 1961 in these words: "The Ecumenical Council will reach out and embrace under the widespread wings of the Catholic Church the entire heredity of Our Lord Jesus Christ. Its principal task will be concerned with the condition and modernization (in Italian: *aggiornamento*) of the Church after 20 centuries of life."[2]

Vatican II arranged the documents it produced into three categories by weight as suggested by their titles: "Constitutions," "Decrees," and "Declarations."[3] The weightiest are the Constitutions, of which there are four: "Dogmatic Constitution on the Church (*Lumen Gentium*)," issued on November 21, 1964; "Dogmatic Constitution on Divine Revelation (*Dei Verbum*)" of November 18, 1965; "Constitution on the Sacred Liturgy (*Sacrosanctum Concilium*)" of December 4, 1963; and "Pastoral Constitution on the Church in the Modern World (*Gaudium et Spes*)" of December 7, 1965.

Then there are nine "Decrees," as follows: the "Decree on the Instruments of Social Communication (*Inter Mirifica*)," December 4, 1963; "Decree on Ecumenism (*Unitatis Redintegratio*)," November 21, 1964; "Decree on the Eastern Catholic Churches (*Orientalium Ecclesiarum*)," November 21, 1964; "Decree on the Bishops' Pastoral Office in the Church (*Christus Dominus*)," October 28, 1965; "Decree on Priestly Formation (*Optatam Totius*)," October 28, 1965; "Decree on the Appropriate Renewal of Religious Life (*Perfectae Caritatis*)," October 28, 1965; "Decree on the Apostolate of the Laity (*Apostolicam Actuositatem*)," November 18, 1965; "Decree on the Ministry and Life of Priests (*Presbyterorum Ordinis*)," December 7, 1965; and "Decree on the Church's Missionary Activity (*Ad Gentes*)," December 7, 1965.

Finally, there are three "Declarations": "Declaration on Christian Education (*Gravissimum Educationis*)," October 28, 1965; "Declaration on the Relationship of the Church to Non-Christian Religions (*Nostra Aetate*)," October 28, 1965; and "Declaration on Religious Freedom (*Dignitatis Humanae*)," December 7, 1965.

The Council held four sessions in all. The first session lasted from October 11 to December 8, 1962; the second from September 29 to December 4, 1963; the third between September 14 and November 21, 1964; and the concluding session between September 14 and December 8, 1965.

---

2. See "Aggiornamento." In The Wikipedia encyclopedia. Accessed November 14, 2016. http://en.wikipedia.org/wiki/Aggiornamento

3. For what follows, see Abbott and Gallagher, *The Documents of Vatican II*, 1966.

Gaudium et Spes is the longest and probably most discussed of the Conciliar documents. By all analyses, it was also the most "outgoing" in terms of *aggiornamento* and *rapprochement*, thus perhaps capturing best Pope John XXIII's overall vision. According to many of the historians of the Council, such as Norman Tanner[4] and John W. O'Malley,[5] it has been the most discussed and generally the most positive of the documents, within and outside the Church. The shortest of the documents are *Inter Mirifica* and *Nostra Aetate*.

It is interesting to note that none of the Council's documents were promulgated before Pope John XXIII, the convener of the Council, died on June 3, 1963. It fell on his successor, Pope Paul VI, to oversee the Council to its solemn conclusion. October 28, 1965 must also have been the "busiest" day of the Council in terms of the official signing of Conciliar documents when five of them were officially ratified. Four were promulgated on December 7, 1965; three on November 21, 1964; and two each on December 4, 1963 and November 18, 1965. The last year of the Council, 1965, saw the promulgation of most of the Conciliar documents, eleven in all.

On account of the tension of perspectives that we have noted among the bishops, there was, of course, significant divergence during the process of preparing and finalizing each of the documents. Some went through several revisions and numerous emendations at every step. Not everything that was prepared by the Drafting or Preparatory Commissions (called *schemas*) was therefore accepted by the Fathers, although some of the Commissions had at first thought and behaved as final drafters. But the actual Conciliar process took on its own (sometimes unexpected) pulse, refusing to simply rubber-stamp the schemas. Not even Pope John XXIII and then Pope Paul VI could themselves always impose their will on the course of events. There were disagreements among the Fathers, among the theologians, and even between the Fathers and theologians. There were also alignments, some of them strategic, among and between these groups. Yet, in the end, the Conciliar texts were approved in the best interests of the faith of the Church. The spirit with which Pope John XXIII had convened the Council prevailed as he had anticipated in his opening speech on October 11, 1962 in St. Peter's Basilica.

Pope John XXIII wanted the Council to be marked by optimism in the loving care of God and by loyal innovation. The pastoral duty of the Bishops in the Church, he had said, is not only to conserve doctrine, "as though it were some museum-piece and we the curators, but earnestly and fearlessly to dedicate ourselves to the work that needs to be done,"[6] keeping the truth of

---

4. Tanner, *Councils of the Church*, 2001.
5. O'Malley, *What Happened at Vatican II*, 2008.
6. Catholic Culture Organization, "Opening Address To the Council by Pope John

the teaching of the Church intact but expressing it in ever new forms as demanded by the times. In all of this, the goal of the Church is to offer to people "the light of Christ," so that human beings may appreciate their dignity before God and hence their calling to justice and charity.

For Africa, *Nostra Aetate*, *Gaudium et Spes*, *Ad Gentes*, and *Dignitatis Humanae*, would later probably have the profoundest impact on the Church there. The openness to the world of *Gaudium et Spes*, which had at first concerned some European bishops and weighty German theologians like Karl Rahner and Joseph Ratzinger, was finally overcome. The last to be promulgated, this document was accepted by 2,309 Fathers as against seventy-two after a "tortuous" and "painful" process, as one historian describes it.

That there are values in non-Christian religions was openly affirmed by *Nostra Aetate* (no. 2) and *Ad Gentes* (no. 22). These would provide the hinge from which African theologians would soon afterwards begin to persistently uncover God-given values in African spirituality and religion. The respect for other religious traditions that *Dignitatis Humane* encouraged for would not escape the attention of Christians rooted in the soil of African Religion. So, in spite of Africa's conspicuous absence at Vatican II as an event, something happened for the Church in Africa and continent from that assembly as an ongoing process.

XXIII." catholicculture.org., accessed April 27, 2016, https://www.catholicculture.org/culture/library/view.cfm?recnum=3233.

Chapter 3

The Holy Spirit at Work

THERE IS NO QUESTION about the subsequent impact of Vatican II on Africa. Because of the Council, major developments have taken place in the Church in Africa since 1965. Both the text and the spirit of Vatican II have facilitated major shifts in the theological, structural, and pastoral understanding and practice of the Church in the continent that would certainly not have been possible without them. The shifts have involved visible structures as well as attitudes. Bishop Michael Ntuyahaga of Bujumbura, Burundi, speaking for the regional bishops during one of the sessions of the Council, intuitively previewed and summarized them when he referred to the "transition" in Churches in Africa from a situation of mission to the status "of young Churches, which are autonomous and exist in their own right." Surely, the Holy Spirit has been at work affirming Vatican II in the Church in Africa.

Looking at developments within the Church in Africa, it is easy to distinguish the structural shifts that have influenced, and actually determined, changes in attitudes there. If there was no adequate African Episcopal representation to make a significant difference during the Council debates, this gradually changed within Africa soon after. Pope Paul VI began to appoint many indigenous bishops to oversee African dioceses, and more and more of these were being created. Many African countries were becoming politically independent and so the appointment of indigenous bishops seemed the necessary and right thing to do. The question of an autonomous Church in Africa in terms of leadership was in many Africans' mind, and it was sometimes expressed aloud by some African Christian politicians. It was to be expected that as African countries became self-governing, people would wonder about the continued governance of the Church by an expatriate hierarchy.

Some visionary missionary bishops stepped aside on their own accord during this period and suggested to Rome their indigenous successors. Bishop Joseph Blomjous of Mwanza, Tanzania, was one of them. Indigenous succession in Church leadership was facilitated at this time also by the increasing number of local clergy in the various dioceses of the continent. Missionary Religious Institutes of both men and women had in general not as yet dared to open their doors to local vocations on a large scale. This might have been a blessing in disguise, for it enabled the natural, cultural attention of the indigenous diocesan clergy and local women's congregations to stay trained on local conditions, even if their actual formal academic training and pastoral formation for a long time remained completely Tridentine and Eurocentric for both. Nevertheless, the formation experience of the diocesan priests and religious (brothers and sisters) could not escape intuitively taking some African local realities into account. African popular theology, the reception and interpretation of Scripture, dogma and other Church teachings by African converts in their own milieu had to be noticed by African diocesan clergy and religious who, basically though covertly, sympathized with it.

Connected with this was the increasing number of converts to Catholicism in the decades of the 1960s and '70s. The parish structure in place since the introduction of Christianity in the sub-continent in the nineteenth century was breaking at the seams, forcing the division of parishes into numerous "out-stations," and later, after the 1970s, into Small Christian Communities (SCCs) in various dioceses. All of these locations could not be staffed and adequately served by ordained priests. Parishes had consequently to depend more and more on lay ministries, such as those of the Catechists, extraordinary ministers of Holy Communion, ministers for the sick, and so on. Up to the present time, however, many of these ministries are unfortunately still not accorded full recognition by many members of the African hierarchy. In fact, they are often viewed with suspicion, thus retarding the development of the theology of SCCs as the new way of being Church. With the notable exception of some dioceses in South Africa, the ministry of permanent (married) deacons has not been accepted with much enthusiasm across the continent, despite the obvious need for this ministry in many dioceses as well as the clear green light given by Rome for its renewal as an institution in the Church. Still, small as it was, the existence of the active participation of the laity in the ministries of the Church as catechists and so on was a clear structural shift set in motion specifically by Vatican II's Decree on the Apostolate of the Laity, *Apostolicam Actuositatem*.

Structural shifts like these were profoundly significant, triggering profound attitudinal changes whose development is still ongoing. Since the Roman Synod on Evangelization in 1974, whose deliberations Pope Paul VI summarized in the Apostolic Exhortation, *Evangelii Nuntiandi*, this experience of change has been considered under four essential headings, usually described—initially by Protestant missiologists—as constituting marks of a genuine local or indigenous Church, namely: self-governance, self-reliance, self-propagating and self-reflecting. The relationship among these requirements and the shifts in the structural reality of the Church bear implications deeper than merely external and organizational.

Overriding other implications as far as attitudes are concerned is the relationship within the communion of the Universal Church. What is the status of the Church in Africa with reference to other Churches in other parts of the world? The question is particularly relevant with regard to the Churches of the northern hemisphere which introduced the Gospel into the southern regions of the African continent. Is the relationship still that of "daughter-to-mother Churches," with its implied emotional, psychological and financial implications of seniority-juniority or superiority-inferiority and dependence on the part of the latter? Or should the relationship be rather that of "sister Churches" with the implications of mutual partnership and complementarity? What is the meaning of the Church in Africa being seen as a "mission" Church? Often inwardly adversarial, the feeling here was a cry for recognition of the identity and adulthood of the Church in Africa as a local Church, with its particular responses to the particular questions facing it at the levels of organization, understanding of the faith, worship, and so on. Of course, the cry has not been completely heeded yet, not even to a satisfactory extent. But the fact that it is widely noticed in Africa itself and beyond is due to the shifts made possible by Vatican II.

Thus, self-governance is understood in the Church in Africa today to involve much more than the presence of indigenous bishops, priests, and religious in positions of leadership in the Church. The more important consideration is what kind of mentality these leaders hold in terms of the African content of their theology and methods of governance. At the end of the day, the jury is still out on this one; it is not clear in actual pastoral practice where the majority of African bishops, priests, and religious stand on issues of vital importance for the Church in Africa. And it is true also to some extent with formally trained catechists. These include questions about the relationship of the Church with civil authorities in terms of human rights and good governance. Is the institutional Church prophetic enough in this matter? There are also concerns internal to the Church itself: theological and pastoral considerations on married clergy, women in ordained ministry, the theology of marriage in Africa, and forms of worship. Does independence of theological imagination necessary for genuine theological, ecclesial, and ecclesiastical contextualization exist in Africa that distinguishes the Church in Africa in these crucial matters from others, taking into account the conditions of life of the Church in Africa?

Respect for and fealty or "submission of mind and will" to the traditional positions of the Church explaining the meaning of the faith in these matters is certainly extremely important in the interests of the unity or oneness of the Universal Church. Nevertheless, it should not and cannot be at the expense of local theological and pastoral reflection and transformation relevant to the needs of the particular Church. When convoking the Council, Pope John XXIII emphasized the necessity for the insertion of the theological and pastoral outlook of the Church at any given time into a particular context. The Church must always reform itself, *ecclesia semper reformanda*. And when the context of the particular Church is as huge as an entire continent or large cultural segments of it, the task becomes much more urgent—and complex.

Here we encounter the very fundamental question of balance in interpretation ("discerning the fruit of the Spirit") between the ongoing work of the Holy Spirit in Church leadership on the one hand, and in the general faithful on the other. It is a necessary dynamic that has always formed the very existence of the Church. The process is not, as is sometimes wrongly perceived, an issue of necessary conflict, of a pernicious struggle between hierarchy and the rest of the faithful. These are not polar opposites since it is the same Spirit working in both. It is, on the contrary, rather an issue of the recognizing the *sensus ecclesiae* or *sensus fidelium,* the sense of wholesome faith of the entire community called Church, both leaders and the rest of the faithful. It is a question of being aware of the very life of the Church itself—the Teaching Church (*ecclesia docens*) and the Listening Church (*ecclesia discens*). The interpretation and correct grasp of the work of the Holy Spirit in the Church, in as far as that happens at any given time, takes place within the dynamics of the understanding of the faith by a movement of the entire community of the faith.

This predisposition is in accord with the Conciliar desire for collegial oversight of the Church. The Council's understanding of the Church as "the People of God" (*Lumen Gentium*, 9–17), is basic. Recently amplified by the first Special Assembly of the Synod of Bishops on Africa (the First African Synod of 1994) as "the Church as Family of God," the goal transcends the practice of collegiality within the Universal Church alone; it rather rooted in and is immediately effective within the local Churches. Although local and regional Episcopal bodies have struggled to be accorded theological significance by

Rome, institutionally and structurally, they would serve very well the collegial desire implied by the Council. But they must first put seriously into practice the principle of listening to the voice of the Spirit working within their own Churches and bringing this to the attention of the Universal Church. Fortunately, Pope Francis has seriously initiated theological and structural movements in this direction. Listening necessitates continual attention to human experience: namely "the joys and the hopes, the grief and the anxieties" of the people, "especially those who are poor or in any way afflicted." This kind of attention can happen only at the grassroots, local level.

Self-propagation of the Church in Africa as an attitude implies, therefore, the development of a contextual theology which takes into account the dynamic relationship between the text of the Gospel, the traditions of the Church hitherto available to us, and the particular African context: its history, physical and social environment, and culture. This implies "inculturation" (also referred to as "enculturation" or "intercultural dialogue") in all of its branches and levels. At the same time, it implies liberation, especially liberation from the structural, intellectual, and spiritual bondage of failing to see and appropriate the presence of God in the human experience of the particular African context. Inculturation is nothing other than living according to the impulses of the Spirit of life, revealed in the communal experience of a people. It involves observing and articulating from the lived experience of a culture, the divine values connected most clearly with the life-enhancing message of Jesus Christ in a way that gives these values flesh in the here and now. Briefly, this is what the spirit of Vatican II was all about.

In Africa, it gave impetus to an awareness that had faintly already begun a decade earlier in the 1950s, pertaining to whether the language and symbols used to express the values of life in the Spirit brought by Jesus were really relevant to the African experience. Why was it deemed necessary to bypass, or worse, denounce, indigenous language and symbols in Christian catechesis and liturgy? The birth of professional African Theology with its recognition of Africa's history and the affirmation of African identity was a consequence of these questions. It was obviously accelerated by both the structural and attitudinal changes that arose in the wake of Vatican II. If there is one gift that emerged from the spirit of the Council which Africa can genuinely celebrate, it is the possibilities that it opened up for the development of African Theology. Just as European theology made possible the revolution that was Vatican II, African Theology is determining a revolutionary shape of the Church of the future in Africa.

The two synods of Africa, in 1994 and 2009, and the apostolic exhortations following each of them in 1996 and 2011, respectively issued by Popes

John Paul II and Benedict XVI, attest to the importance of African Theology for the development of the Church in the continent. Although the "magisterial status" of African Theology has not as yet been fully employed by the African episcopate at the service of the Church in Africa, its influence is nonetheless evident in the synodal discussions, the Propositions of the Bishops to the Popes, and finally in the two exhortations we have referred to. But the question remains: even with its influence at these levels of the Church, how do the insights of African Theology reach the Church in Africa in general, the *ecclesia discerns*—at the Parish and Small Christian Community levels where the Church should be experienced as such? The Papal Exhortations, *Ecclesia in Africa* by Pope John Paul II and *Africae Munus* by Pope Benedict XVI may contain indispensable theological orientations for the Church in Africa of the present and future, but they will have no effect in this regard unless they are received by all the faithful and lived out by them.

It takes deliberate organization and planning to bring about intelligent reception of Church teaching: the message must reach its intended audience, in this case, the general faithful. It is on the level of method to bring this realization about that the issue of self-reliance comes to the fore. It is not possible for the local Church to be genuinely self-governing and self-propagating if it is not self-reliant. The Church in Africa has had a long-standing experience of dependency and is familiar with its consequences of humiliation and theological and pastoral stagnation. On the practical, empirical level, neither African dioceses nor parishes can start any development program without financial donations from European and American Churches, so that if this aid is not forthcoming the projects are stillborn or shelved. In terms of the self-identity and dignity of a particular Church in this situation, the practical and psychological consequences can be tragic, as they have been in many parts of Africa. Some of these translate into total abdication of responsibility for one's life.

But there have been problems in the Church in Africa *vis-a-vis* Vatican II as well. One of these may be described as the situation of "reception without analysis." While the spirit of the Council is clearly visible in the transformation of the structures and attitudes in the Church, it is largely not consciously streamlined in order to further more profound and orderly theological and pastoral horizons inherent in, but not fully articulated or realized by the Council itself. Of course, being a global event, the Council could not do this, nor did it intend to do so. That responsibility was left up to each local or particular Church. Vatican II, furthermore, has been described not as a doctrinal but as a Pastoral Council. It was not convoked to offer pointed answers to specific problems worldwide, as were the first several Ecumenical Councils, or even the two modern Councils of Trent and Vatican I. Respectively, the latter were concerned about the Protestant Reformation and Papal infallibility. Unlike these Councils, however, Vatican II was an invitation to current and future generations to read the signs of God's activity in the world so that the Catholic faithful, and indeed "all people of goodwill," would embrace this activity and appropriate it for the sake of harmony, peace, and joy of the world.

The intention of Pope John XXIII was to make Vatican II a see-through window, for those outside the Church to look in and those inside to look out. Gradually, this is happening in the Church in Africa, but the process must be sustained.

Chapter 4

Collegial Leadership in the Church in Africa

WHO (OR WHAT) IS the Church? This is a perennial question. Theoretically it may seem settled but in practice it remains quite frustrating. In Africa, it is crucial for the realization of the spirit of Vatican II.

Theologically, the leaders together with all baptized faithful form the Body of Christ. Further analogies like the People of God and Family of God point to the profundity of this insight. Structurally, however, great difficulty exists in realizing this theological assertion, from the very basic level of Small Christian Communities (SCCs), to parish and diocesan organization, to the structure and relationship between and among the particular and local Churches on the universal level. The question concerns the meaning and implications of leadership or "hierarchy" in the Church—one of the most entrenched but also misinterpreted and misused notions in Church governance.

The notion receives thorough explanation in Vatican II's Dogmatic Constitution on the Church, *Lumen Gentium* (no. 18–29). Here, great emphasis is placed on the practical organization of the Church, with the language of "governors" and "helpers" applied, for example, to bishops and priests and deacons. About the appropriateness or otherwise of such language and attendant attitudes, a lot has been written. Certainly abuses have occurred even in the post-conciliar history of the Church on account of various practical interpretations made of it. Amidst all that, the true spirit of hierarchy as elaborated by the Council appears clearly in statements like this one: "pastors, selected to shepherd the Lord's flock, are servants of Christ and stewards of the mysteries of God. To them has been assigned the bearing of witness to the Gospel of God's grace and to the ministration of the Spirit and of God's glorious power to make men just" (no. 21).

From this it seems obvious that the proper understanding and use of hierarchy is for the goal of service and unity in the Church. It is not primarily a matter of status. The latter, although it can also be gleaned from this Conciliar document, is nevertheless not its primary purpose. Jesus, the proto-priest, came not to be served but to serve and to lay down his life for his sheep (John 10:11–18). The same charge was given to Peter: "Feed my sheep" (see John 21:15–17). The ecclesiological question of hierarchy in Africa, simply put, is therefore this: What is the relationship between SCC leaders or ministers and the parish priest, between the parish priest and the bishop, and between the bishop and the Pope? More precisely, how should their functions be coordinated? Does collegiality extend to this entire range of leadership in the Church? The Council initiated radical changes here too.

The organization of the Council itself began to deemphasize the previous strong distinction between bishops and theologians, since many bishops depended on their theologians for advice for their submissions. A form of "equality"—at least in terms of the working of the Holy Spirit—was thereby perhaps inadvertently being practiced here. Once the Spirit's presence was recognized in the theologians, it could not be limited to them, but had to be accepted as present and valid in other faithful too, each in his or her own capacity. God could speak directly not only to the bishops and other ordained leaders in the Church but to anyone He chose. The circular image of the Church as the People of God rather than the pyramidal one of "lords and serfs" began to emerge and gather momentum.

To actualize this nascent sense of collegiality that was palpable in the entire Conciliar process, necessitating dialogue, communion, and service, Pope Paul VI took a drastic measure. On September 15, 1965 by his personal initiative (*motu proprio*) he published the document *Apostolica Sollicitudo* detailing the institution of the Synod of Bishops as a permanent structure in the organization of the Church. Two subsequent Extraordinary General Assemblies of Bishops in 1969 and 1985 respectively confirmed Pope Paul VI's vision that the main goal for the synods should be the collaboration by all the faithful in "governing" the Church. This explains why, since their institution, the synods were required to involve as many faithful as possible in their preparation, especially the laity. The sense of the faithful for each synod ought to be sought at the crucial stage of preparation of the working document. The ordinary and extraordinary general synods involving the Universal Church have tried to be faithful to this principle.

Of singular interest in this structure have been the particular or special synods. These are convened to address an issue facing a given local Church or one in the context of that Church, avoiding general answers (or grand stories) thought applicable to the entire Global Church. But if there were universal answers proposed, they arose from concrete experiences of a given local Church. The special assembly for Asia in 1998 is a case in point. On account of the plurality, diversity, and strength of the Asian religions, and the very small presence of Christians compared to the general population in that continent, it was important to address and highlight the theme of the uniqueness of Jesus Christ in the divine economy of salvation among these religions. Because of a different demography, a theme like this would not be necessary for other continents.

Africa's two special assemblies in 1994 and 2009 respectively had as themes Evangelization—"The Church in Africa and Her Evangelizing Mission towards the Year 2000: 'You Shall Be My Witnesses' (Acts 1:8)" and Justice and Peace—"The Church in Africa in Service to Reconciliation, Justice and Peace: 'You Are the Salt of the Earth . . . You Are the Light of the World' (Mt. 5:13, 14)." In the African situation, both of these continue to be pressing issues from which the Church cannot turn away.

As the First African Synod was taking place, the genocide in Rwanda was happening. The second assembly was held against the backdrop of massive corruption and civil strife in many African countries, leading to the phenomenon of failed states in the case of several of them. The anarchical situation characterizing failing or failed states was accompanied by massive internal and external displacement of people, abuse of human freedoms and rights, and misuse of resources. It has led the continent of Africa into deeper anthropological poverty and the marginalization of many of its states from meaningful participation in the life of the world community of nations.

The work of the synods so far has sprung from the realization that structures of human freedom and dignity are inherently part of God's work of saving the world. Taking the two special synods on Africa, this is clearly what is being attempted. Inculturation featured prominently as a central theme of the first because of the rise of awareness of the importance of African culture in authentic evangelization if faith is to be integrated authentically with the life or the "deep structure" of African thought. The gap that exists between the current expressions of faith in Christ clothed mainly in Western cultural language and the African spiritual worldview, creating a kind of double religious existence among African Christians, must be overcome. The Second Synod's emphasis on justice, reconciliation and peace captured the yearning and cry of the African poor who are oppressed, not only internally by corrupt leaders, but also externally by international structures of injustice. But true Christian faith cannot exist without justice, nor can human communion be achieved without peace. Both sets of realities are intertwined. Proposition 14 of the propositions of the synod describes justice as "the fruit of reconciliation between God and humanity, and within the human family itself." Community and communion are realized in justice and reconciliation.

The changed self-perception of the Church and the new "circular" pastoral perspective initiated by Vatican II necessitates a new approach to mission. Rapid developments in human society and their impact on the environment made inevitable the question of how to do mission, or how the Church can be mission in the twenty-first century.

Chapter 5

Singing about God in an African Key

IN REFERENCE TO THE North American Church, theologian Mary E. Hines identifies several needs, or what she terms "impulses," discernible in the development of the Church there since the end of Vatican II. They include acceptance in the Church of freedom of theological research, the role of women, the contribution of lay theologians, and the necessity of ecumenical and interreligious dialogue.[1] Similar impulses characterize the Church in Africa as well, in the continent's own particular circumstances.

By the middle of this century, we will be celebrating the centenary of the birth of African Theology, which, in its professional sense, can be traced to three moments: the publication by Placide Tempels of his book, *Philosophie bantoue* in 1945, the publication of a collection of reflections by African and Haitian priests as *Des pretres noirs s'interrogent* in 1956, and the debate in Kinshasa in 1960 on the relevance of "African Theology" between Prof. Alfred Vanneste and his erstwhile student Tharcisse Tshibangu.

In their reflections, the African and Haitian priests questioned the relevance, to Africa and the African people, of the idiom in which the Christian faith was being presented. Their reflections were certainly given impetus by the work of the Belgian missionary priest in the Congo, Tempels, who, about eleven years earlier had argued that black Africans south of the Sahara had a distinctive worldview about life and God. He implied that this worldview should be respected and used in the transmission of the Gospel. To this

---

1. See Mary E. Hunt, "North American 'Impulses' following Vatican II" in *Concilium* 3, 107.

end, he founded the *Jamaa* (or family) movement in 1953, which at its peak numbered almost 200,000 people. The intuition and methods of the movement were precursors of the Small Christian Communities, introduced and endorsed later in many parts of the sub-Saharan region by the hierarchy. The emphasis in both rested on regular meetings and mutual assistance based on the African communal view of life. Tempels, or "Baba Placide," as he was affectionately called, continued to inspire the movement long after he had left the Congo for Belgium.

This, as might be expected, did not go well with the thinking of many missionaries at the time. According to available reports, "the most serious" objection against Tempel's ideas came from within the Church's hierarchy itself in the country. Monsignor Jean Felix de Hemptinne, the Catholic Bishop of Elizabethville (now Lubumbashi) argued that the term "civilization" could not be applied to black people given the reality that they could not write. For him, Tempels, whom he described as "the little Capuchin," was a troublemaker. De Hemptinne tried his best to engineer the fall of Tempels by bringing his person and work to an unfavorable attention with the authorities in Rome. Fortunately, however, Tempels enjoyed the support and encouragement of several important people, including the respected Cardinal Joseph Cardijn, founder and director of the Young Christian Workers Movement, the highly influential Jesuit professor of missiology at Louvain, Pierre Charles, and the widely read author and diplomat, Chinese Benedictine Dom Celestin Lou.

But if de Hemptinne's was the typical view in the Catholic Church in Africa during the period before Vatican II, it began to change after the Council on account of the Council's opening the Church's windows for development of local Churches and theologies. By the late 1960s, Pope Paul VI was explicit about this need. He not only called for an African Theology but an African Church. Subsequent Popes articulated the same need. However, this development has been slow. Even after these endorsements and those by the two African synods, African theologians have not received sufficient support for their work from the African hierarchy itself. They seem to be hemmed in by cautions and strictures in their research unwarranted by the spirit of the Council. The "danger of syncretism and relativism" is the red cards always waved before them. Perhaps most affected of all are women and lay theologians.

One of the most vexing issues that will continue to face the Universal Catholic Church in the days ahead concerns women in ordained ministry. Many officials in the Church continue to argue that reserving ordained ministry exclusively to men is Jesus' own mandate and the Church "has no power" to change it. But mounting understanding of Scripture, sociology, and psychology, and practical changes in the civil sphere seem to contradict this stance. Current developments point to grave shortcomings in previous stereotypes about gender that were once seen as divine will. For the Church in this matter, biology or gender seem to be considered as destiny. African Women's Theology is on the cutting edge of change in theological thinking in this and other issues.

Attentive to the Church and African culture, African women theologians critically analyze both and point out religious and cultural elements in belief and practice that are contradictory to the Gospel of Christ. In this way, they constructively challenge both the Church and African culture in terms of human rights and the demands of justice. They see their task as to bring women and men together as God's family so as to witness to the common dignity of all human beings and to be solicitous about the rights of God's creation entrusted to them. African women theologians underline the imperative not to carelessly dominate and expropriate nature but to nurture it for the sake of sharing the life-giving divine Spirit within it.

With the patriarchal tendencies still in place in the Church and in African communities, African Women's Theology has not received unanimous universal approval in the continent. Many criticize and even condemn it as un-African culturally, and even anti-Church or anti-Gospel theologically.

In Africa, women theologians are lay or religious. The former work in public institutions and so are relatively "independent" from direct control of the bishops. This is different from African male theologians, the majority of whom are still clerics. The African women theologians who are religious may, despite the theological position of the bishop, continue doing theology under the "protection" of their religious orders, especially if these Institutes or Congregations are international. Under such protection, the process of dialogue between the two parties, the theologian and the bishop, may continue, sometimes leading to the vindication of the position of the theologian in question or to mutual understanding between the two sides.

Abuse of power by members of the hierarchy against theological charism sometimes happens regardless of the best of intentions by the individuals in authority. There is evidence of incidences of this in the long history of the Church. It is part of the sinful aspect of the Church, to be continually cleansed in its present pilgrimage in the world. The consequences of abuse of power are always negative to the Church-institution in that they stunt its growth in terms of openness to new breath of the divine Spirit which comes about only when creative tension between charisms is carefully and deliberately maintained.

It is not helpful when ulterior motives are imputed on a theologian, that his or her reflection is nothing else but a search for personal fame and glory. Not only is this unhelpful, it is unethical. It is unhelpful because that is always an argument *ad hominem* that fails or refuses to engage the theological reflection itself. It can be used against anyone with whom one does not agree. It is unethical and morally dangerous because the question of motivation belongs to a person's internal forum. Its evaluation is best left between the individual and God.

Vatican II placed considerable emphasis on ecumenical and interreligious dialogue. It is no exaggeration to say that it is also partly on this emphasis that the novelty of the Council lies. If there was any conspicuous break by Vatican II with the past, it was in this area as well. Since the later patristic period, the tendency had been to defend the Church at any cost against any other (new) teaching. After the Reformation the predisposition became, in addition, to reject any different expression of the Truth of Christ but that approved by the *Roman Catholic Church* alone. Vatican II, however, transcended these two positions and affirmed the presence of the seeds of the Truth of God in other faiths and other Christian denominations. How has the Church in Africa appropriated this insight of the Council in its dealings with other Christian Churches—and African Religion in particular?

Dialogue with African Religion is of special importance because African spirituality forms the basis of Christian living for the vast majority of African Christians. There is universal recognition of this fact, but uncertainty dominates in how to proceed. On account of its long nurture in the western world and in Greco-Roman philosophy, there is in some minds an identification of this historical development with divine fiat. Nothing must be "tampered" with; things must always remain the same (*semper idem*). This mentality and attitude undervalue the self-revelation of God in African culture. It tends to make of inculturation a very superficial exercise. It does not allow a radical examination of Christ's message within the context of African history and experience to which the spirit of Vatican II points and genuine inculturation demands.

For many centuries, the Church judged the world as if it existed outside of it. The dominant paradigm of Church councils was warning or condemnation of those who thought or behaved differently (heretics). All truth was considered to be concentrated in the Catholic Church. But Vatican II called for change. Instead of unmitigated judgment of everything secular, the Council urged attentiveness to the possibility of finding the divine voice also in the world. Instead of unremitting condemnation of the "different other," the Council advocated pastoral understanding and sympathy. Instead of the position that the Catholic Church alone possesses the whole truth, the Council acknowledged that other religious traditions and faiths also contain some rays of divine revelation from which the Church can learn through mutually respectful dialogue. Instead of the position that error has no rights, Vatican II recognized that all human beings, indeed all elements of creation, are on pilgrimage towards the wholeness of the divine who beckons every creature forward to himself. On the journey sometimes people falter. What is important is untiring fraternal correction.

The forces of change in the Church Vatican II so quietly unleashed cannot be completely exhausted. In Africa, these forces must be directed at some specific goals. When Pope Benedict XVI dedicated the period between October 11, 2012 and November 24, 2013 as the "Year of Faith," urging Catholics, among other things, to reread the documents of the Council, perhaps this is what he intended for the Universal Church. In dedicating the period between December 8, 2015 and November 20, 2016 as the "Year of Mercy," perhaps Pope Francis intended the same thing. The impact of the Council lies in the hands of action, to realize its ideals.

How can this be done effectively in the days and years ahead in the African context?

Above all, every adult Catholic Christian must assume the responsibility to search for oneself before God what true faith means in one's life. Even though living the faith has an inalienable communitarian dimension, the personal responsibility in understanding and applying it in personal life cannot be transferable. "To rediscover the content of the faith that is professed, celebrated, lived and prayed, and to reflect on the act of faith, is a task that every believer must make his [or her] own."[2] In this task Vatican II cannot be bypassed; it remains an important tool for personal and Church renewal. For the African local Church, the foundational catechetical induction as well as the ongoing formation into the faith must be based explicitly on the documents of the Council. In this, African Theology will play an important role.

---

2. Benedict XVI, '*Motu Proprio Data' Porta Fidei*. Encyclical Letter, Vatican Website, October 11, 2011, http://www.vatican.va/holy_father/benedict_xvi/apost_exhortations/documents/hf_ben-xvi_exh_20111119_africae-munus_en.html, 9.

Chapter 6

Culture as the Path of Faith

It is relatively easy to retrieve what Vatican II, various Popes since then, the two synods on Africa, as well as many individual bishops throughout the continent have said about the importance of integrating the African religious belief into the Christian message. All of this is summed up nowhere better than in Pope John Paul II's expression that "the synthesis between culture and faith is not only a requirement of culture, but also of faith," and that "faith that does not become culture is not fully accepted, nor entirely reflected upon, or faithfully experienced." Still, prevarication in this process is evident in Africa. So, integrating faith and culture remains one of the most important tasks for the Church in Africa. The spirit of Vatican II will hardly be fully realized without addressing this responsibility.

Pope John Paul II's exhortation in *Ecclesia in Africa* after the First African Synod was a practical call to respect African indigenous religiosity, to avoid stereotyping it negatively, and to instruct future Christian leaders into a judicious appreciation of its values. The crucial question is how many dioceses or Episcopal conferences have done this, so many years after this call? How many have established courses in African Religion in houses of formation for priests and religious? How many are ready to single out knowledgeable African Christian elders who could provide the Church with this insider appreciation?

Since Vatican II the Popes have been almost relentless in underlining the importance of culture as the context of evangelization. In 1982, Pope John Paul II explained to the bishops of Nigeria in Lagos that *"the path of culture is the path of man,* and it is on this path that man encounters the One who embodies the values of all cultures and fully reveals the man of each culture to himself." The Pope went on to specify that "the Gospel of Christ the Incarnate Word finds its home along the path of culture and from this path it continues to offer its message of salvation and eternal life."[1] Here Pope John Paul II was echoing the sentiments of his predecessor, Pope Paul VI. The same feelings have later been articulated even more strongly by Pope Benedict XVI and Pope Francis.

This deep concern of the Popes refers to the need for theology, catechesis, and pastoral ministry, and the Church in general to be meaningful to people, so as to communicate effectively the Good News of Jesus Christ. Rather than import methods and practices of Church from outside, it is necessary to have them home grown. In the words of the great Protestant theologian Paul Tillich, which the counsel of Pope John Paul II echoes, the Christian evangelization must realize that "religion is the substance of culture and culture is the form of religion."[2]

Since the early centuries of Christianity in northern Africa, the theological positions that have influenced thinking in this area have consisted in radical discontinuity between culture and the Christian message on the one hand, and judicious continuity between them on the other. The first opinion was championed by Tertullian, who was convinced that philosophy had nothing whatsoever to offer to the process of understanding the Gospel. He expressed this conviction in his famous question: "What . . . has Athens to do with Jerusalem? What concord is there in the Academy and the Church?" Contrary to this conviction was that of the equally theologically astute Clement of Alexandria. According to Clement, "Philosophy is in a sense a work of Divine Providence. . . . The Greek preparatory culture . . . with philosophy itself, is shown to have come down from God to man."[3] The historical sense of the Church seems to have taken the side of Clement.

Already in the mid-seventeenth century, the Sacred Congregation of the Propagation of the Faith instructed missionaries not to force people to change their cultural ways if these did not manifestly go against the Gospel. In the classical advise of the congregation, "do not in any way attempt and do not on any pretext persuade these people to change their rites, habits and customs, unless they are openly opposed to religion and good morals." The congregation described this method of evangelization as "absurd." "For what could be

---

1. See http://afrikaworld.net/afrel/atr-popes.html.
2. See Tienou, *Theological Task of the Church*, 24.
3. See Tienou, *Theological Task of the Church*, 21.

more absurd than to bring France, Spain, Italy or any other European country to China," or Africa, for that matter?[4]

In different words and ways, the founders of several missionary organizations aimed at the evangelization of Africa voiced similar sentiments to their members. Bishop Daniel Comboni of the Comboni Missionaries of the Heart of Jesus or Verona Fathers and Sisters, Cardinal Charles Lavigerie of the Society of the Missionaries of Africa, and Fr. Francis Libermann of the Holy Ghost Fathers may be cited as examples. These had trust in the African people's religiosity and their institutions, leading Comboni, for instance, to coin his famous phrase that it was only possible to "save Africa through Africa." In general, they urged their members to be Africans with the Africans, to eat what they eat, wear what they wear, and as far as possible to live the life the Africans live. But it is well known that these instructions were too often observed in the breach on the ground. What is worse is that the missionaries taught their would-be African collaborators in seminaries and houses of formation to despise African culture. This has been the ultimate drawback to meaningful inculturation.

In many cases, the local clergy, because of the type of education they have received on this issue, appear to be intellectually alienated from their cultural realities. They are deeply suspicious of African cultural practices. Emotionally, however, they cannot be completely detached from them and often revert to them in secret. This is a cause of considerable mental and spiritual stress for those concerned. The African Initiated Churches have tried to confront this situation in their members, in many instances without an elaborate theology of contextualization.

Contextual theology questions the idea of a "universal theology" in the sense of a theology applicable everywhere in a uniform manner, regardless of culture and language. It is also suspicious of the idea of complete "objectivity" of any theologian. Contextual theology argues from the perspective that if theology is principally human interpretation of the reality of God, it is necessarily a "point of view": different people can legitimately see, understand, and interpret God differently. Cultures and the physical and social environments in which different people live and in which theology is done, greatly influence the perception and interpretation of the great divine reality. In one way or another, they condition its particular appropriation and understanding.

The contextual process involves two essential dynamics. On the one hand, it calls for continual reassessment of theological reflection and pastoral practice within the Church in a given context. The question here is how far the life of the particular Christian community is in conformity with current

---

4. See Neuner and Dupuis, *The Christian Faith*, 309.

understanding of the demands of the Gospel, given the prevailing social-cultural, political, and economic environment around them. This question is linked directly to another, whose aim is to foster total human liberation under the guidance of the word of God. On this dimension, contextual theology places these human realities continually under the scrutiny of the Gospel so as to determine how much the goal of liberation has been approximated.

The contextual theologian needs to be familiar with both the official Church symbolic, didactic, and ritual language and that of the actual people to whom the Gospel is proclaimed. Are the linguistic and symbolic forms employed in communicating the Gospel appropriate to the concrete life-experience of the people? Thus, theology by this procedure fundamentally emerges from the effort of the community of believers to understand the divine. The vocation of the professional theologian is to assess this experience critically and guide it judiciously. This task of theology is not always foolproof. It can make many errors on account of the always finite penetrability of human intelligence into the totality of the Divine Being. This is why, in interpreting the meaning and requirements of the Gospel, the theologian must continuously pay attention to constructive tension between popular appropriation of the faith and the official teaching of the Church. It requires on the part of the theologian: a clear awareness of the actual environment or context in which theology is done; knowledge of the intended subjects of the particular theology; self-identity of the theologian or the one who speaks about God; and choice of the means of communicating this theology.[5]

At the end of their meeting in Accra, Ghana in 1977, African theologians articulated the fundamental importance of context in doing theology in a communiqué. They insisted that it implies taking the whole life of the African person as it has been and is being shaped by various historical circumstances into account. For them, "African theology must be understood in the context of African life and culture and the creative attempt of African peoples to shape a new future that is different from the colonial past and the neo-colonial present."[6] Because the history of the continent involves economic and political domination and cultural alienation, contextual African theology must be liberation theology. It must struggle to rehabilitate the values of African culture, often unfairly demonized by different ideologies. In addition, it must today struggle against Africa's own internal demons in the form of political oppression, economic subservience, injustice, and sexism.

Africans cannot come to the Christian faith in a cultural vacuum and should not be expected to. They encounter the Gospel with an awareness of

---

5. See Schreiter, "Foreword," vii–viii.
6. Appiah-Kubi and Torres, *African Theology en Route*, 193.

who they are as Africans, of how their environment and culture have shaped them. A mature faith aided by contextual theology can be founded only on this awareness. Here cultural presuppositions conditioned by the African environment can be realistically challenged by the Gospel. In turn, the Gospel will gain deeper understanding by the African faithful. Important cultural presuppositions will include the following, as Pope Paul VI enumerated them in his message to Africa, *Africae Terrarum* (no. 7–14):

1. "the spiritual view of Life,"
2. "the idea of God,"
3. "respect for human dignity,"
4. "the sense of family," and
5. "community life."

Some of these beliefs and the customs and rites arising from them, "once considered to be strange," the Pope writes, "are seen today, in the light of ethnological science, as integral parts of various social systems, worthy of study and commanding respect."

This same sentiment was expressed by Pope John Paul II in the 1995 Apostolic Exhortation, *Ecclesia in Africa,* after the First African Synod, and by Pope Benedict XVI in *Africae Munus* of 2011, after the Second African Synod. Pope Paul VI had followed his analysis of African values in *Africae Terrarum* by a *cri de coeur* to Africa through the bishops of Africa and Madagascar in 1969, telling the continent in no uncertain terms: "You may, and you must, have an African Christianity. Indeed, you possess human values and characteristic forms of culture which can rise up to perfection such as to find in Christianity, and for Christianity, a true superior fullness, and prove to be capable of a richness of expression all of its own, and genuinely African."[7] The Incarnation of God in Jesus justifies this process. The Incarnation has made possible the personal encounter between human culture and God, thereby adopting or assuming it into the Godhead and redeeming it.

As Vatican II noted in the Pastoral Constitution of the Church in the Modern World, *Gaudium et Spes*, there is a fundamental link between Christian revelation and human culture. God speaks to men and women according to the culture of their time. "The Good News . . . takes the spiritual qualities and endowments of every age and nation" the document says, "and with supernatural riches it causes them to blossom, as it were, from within; it fortifies,

---

7. Paul VI, "Eucharistic Celebration at the Conclusion of the Symposium Organized by the Bishops of Africa: Homily of Paul VI," Kampala (Uganda), 31 July 1969.

completes and restores them in Christ" (no. 58). The Dogmatic Constitution on the Church, *Lumen Gentium*, does not see diversity of cultures as a hindrance to evangelization, but as something positive through which the Holy Spirit works to bring people to the salvation of Christ (no. 13). This is an insight that has been emphasized by Pope Benedict XVI in *Africae Munus* and Pope Francis in *Evangelii Gaudium*.

The Decree on the Missionary Activity of the Church, *Ad Gentes* (no. 22), encourages the Church in each socio-cultural area not to scorn but to take "from the customs and traditions of their people, from their wisdom and their learning, from their arts and disciplines, all those things which can contribute to the glory of their Creator, or enhance the grace of their Savior, or dispose Christian life the way it should be." Pope John Paul II returned to this subject again and again in his numerous letters and messages. In his opinion, the term "Inculturation" expresses "very well one factor of the great mystery of the Incarnation." What evangelization is called to do is to bring the power of the Gospel into the very heart of culture and cultures," according to the Pope in *Catechesi Tradendae* (no. 53), and this can only be done effectively if the agent of evangelization is deeply familiar with the "most significant expressions" of the culture in question.

The responsibility of every missionary of the Gospel is to be "bicultural": not renouncing their own cultural identity, but at the same time immersing themselves into "the environment in which they are working, and therefore of equipping themselves to communicate effectively with it, adopting a manner of living which is a sign of Gospel witness and of solidarity with the people (*Redemptoris Missio*, no. 53). For, as Pope Paul VI put it in *Evangelii Nuntiandi* (no. 20):

> the kingdom which the Gospel proclaims is lived by ... [people] who are profoundly linked to a culture, and the building up of the kingdom cannot avoid borrowing the elements of human culture or cultures. Though independent of cultures, the Gospel and evangelization are not necessarily incompatible with them; rather they are capable of permeating them all without becoming subject to any one of them.

An important fact of inculturation that must be kept in mind is that the subjects to whom the Gospel must be communicated are ever changing. Local theologies are *local* precisely on account of the fact of stability and change. Even though values arising out of local situations can and may be universalized, the reality of change must be recognized. Even within one given context, the situation may not always be homogenous: stories may be perceived differently on the level of individuals. Pastoral theology must take this fact into account so as to be able to offer relevant pastoral care according to the needs of individual persons.

The community reflecting on its experience in the name of Jesus is, in the first instance, "the theologian." But there is a distinct and important role for the professional theologian in the faith-life of the Christian community and a careful balance must be struck between the function and responsibility of each of these entities. If the community creates its own experience of faith, the theologian helps to clarify and direct this experience within the general context of the faith of the entire Universal Church, for the sake of mutuality of the Churches. Thus, the function of the professional theologian within the Christian community cannot be ignored. But the professional theologian must not dominate the community because he or she is also a member of the community, sharing the same experience as the other faithful. Paul's analogy of the different parts of the body applied to the gifts (charisms) in the Church (1 Cor 12:4–30) is most apt.

To be a credible interpreter of the community's spiritual experience and, consequently, an effective communicator of God within the community, the professional theologian needs to fulfill certain conditions. First and foremost, the contextual theologian must be "situated" in the context whose experience he or she wishes to interpret and in which he or she proposes to communicate the Gospel. In other words, the theologian needs to be an "insider" psychosocially. It is essential that the theologian understands and empathizes with the questions the community asks.

Secondly, the contextual theologian must be intellectually trained in the skills of analysis, particularly of the primary sources of the Christian belief: the Bible, the faith tradition of the Universal Church, and the ongoing divine revelation through the community's experience or, in other words, the development of doctrine. The training should prepare the theologian intellectually and psychologically to be open enough so as to avoid theological myopia, a condition which often leads to dangerous parochialism and fundamentalism. What Pope John Paul II openly apologized for on behalf of the entire Church in his message for the Great Jubilee Year of 2000, *Tertio Millenio Adveniente* (no. 35), recognizes the danger of theological short-sightedness, leading to intolerance. In the message, the Pope regrets some missionaries' historical "acquiescence given . . . to *intolerance and even the use of violence* in the service of truth." In his view, "From these painful moments of the past a lesson can be drawn for the future, leading all Christians to adhere fully to the sublime principle stated by the Council: 'The truth cannot impose itself except by virtue of its own truth, as it wins over the mind with both gentleness and power.'"

An important quality of the Christian contextual theologian is serving the particular community in self-awareness that he or she is also serving the Universal Church. Although experiences are expressed differently in different contexts, Christian values are nevertheless similar everywhere because the Spirit of God cannot contradict itself. For this purpose, several documents of the Church and Papal messages have urged African theologians and intellectuals to study African Religion and culture. In *Ecclesia in Africa* (no. 63), Pope John Paul II writes: "It is earnestly to be hoped that theologians in Africa will work out the theology of the Church as Family with all the riches contained in this concept, showing its complementarity with other images of the Church." The responsibility of African Catholic universities in promoting African culture and religion, "by promoting the work of inculturation especially in liturgical celebration, by publishing books and publicizing Catholic truth, by undertaking assignments given by the Bishops and by contributing to a scientific study of cultures" is emphasized equally by Pope John Paul II in *Ecclesia in Africa* (no. 103) and Pope Benedict XVI in *Africae Munus* (no. 136). On this, Pope Benedict XVI (no. 137) expresses a dream for the future of African Theology, that it may experience a renaissance similar to that "of the prestigious School of Alexandria. Why should we not hope that it could furnish today's Africans and the Universal Church with great theologians and spiritual masters who could contribute to the sanctification of the inhabitants of this continent and of the whole Church?"

It is not an unrealistic dream. If in other areas of life Africa produced for the world such illuminating personalities as Nelson Mandela and Julius Nyerere, there is no reason why it cannot happen in the Church in the theological sphere, with committed and courageous individuals. Pope John Paul II was explicit in this matter when addressing some students in Cote d'Ivoire. Recalling the values Pope Paul VI and he himself had enumerated earlier (and adding to the list "the taste for feasts and symbols . . . [and] attachment to dialogue and palaver to settle differences"), he urged the young people to "preserve" and "safeguard" them. He described them as "a real treasure from which you can and must draw something new for the building up of your country, on an original and typically African model, made up of harmony between the values of its cultural past and the most acceptable elements of modern civilization."[8] This and other forms of encouragement contained in the conciliar, synodal, and Episcopal comments on this issue of the dialogue between the Christian faith and African spirituality contain a spirit of genuine concern for the rooting of the faith in Africa and the integrity of the African Christian believer.

---

8. See http://afrikaworld.net.afrel/atr-popes.html.

Doing theology is closely tied up with the economy of revelation, or revelation as we experience it here and now in the world. Both are situated in a context and must be interpreted. That interpretation must be continually revised by using linguistic tools of one kind or another. For theology, the questions are: What is the context where revelation and its interpretation are taking place? Who are the individuals and communities experiencing divine revelation to whom the theologian is accountable? How is the theologian, as an interpreter of divine revelation, situated in the context? Finally, what is the best way by which to bring out what God may be saying to us? As long as divine revelation continues, which is to say as long as humanity exists, the task of doing theology will continue.

Chapter 7

African Paths to Religious Life

THE WORK OF VOCATIONS animators to the religious life is vital for the continued existence of Religious Congregations and Societies. But perhaps even more important, it is work that is essential for the continued existence of the Church as a witness of kingdom values to the world, the values of Faith, Hope, Charity, Justice, Reconciliation, and Peace. This is so on account of the special and specialized charisms that Religious Institutes bring to the Church and through the Church to the entire world. Even a rapid look at the history of Christianity anywhere, but especially in Africa, reveals that without religious communities, of both women and men, the Church's witness of these values, so sorely needed in the continent and the world today, would surely be much less brilliant.

Today, Africa plays a unique role in this regard of witnessing to the Gospel message "even to the very ends of the earth" (Acts 1:8). In the Apostolic Exhortation, *Ecclesia in Africa* (no. 134), Pope John Paul II makes no secret of his joy about the presence of the missionary spirit in the Church in Africa. He writes that it is for him "a source of great comfort to know that the Missionary Institutes which have been present in Africa for a long time are now 'receiving more and more candidates from the young Churches which they founded,' thus enabling these same Churches to take part in the missionary activity of the universal Church" (EA no. 134).

Continuing, the Pope applauds and thanks God "for the new Missionary Institutes which have been established on the continent and are now sending their members *ad gentes*." As the Pope sees it, "this is a providential and marvelous development which shows the maturity and dynamism of the Church in Africa." It is the Pope's view that the missionary spirit that is emerging in Africa is a witness to "the unity of humankind," which begins in the Church itself. "By responding to her vocation to be a redeemed and reconciled people in the midst of the world," the Pope explains, "the Church contributes to promoting the fraternal coexistence of all peoples, since she transcends any human distinctions" (EA no. 137).

Granted that the missionary vocation in the Church in Africa is a *kairos*, an opportune moment to be grateful for to God, it places upon the Church in Africa its own demands in the context of our time and circumstances, one of which is the importance of culture to the missionary vocation in Africa. What role does culture play as individuals offer and dedicate themselves entirely to the service of God, as members of Religious Institutes? What are some of the factors that come into play in the process?

One thing to always keep in mind is that vision precedes practice in the process of mission. More precisely in the Christian context, mission is born out of theology and not vice versa. Any style of mission we engage in reflects the theology we hold. Even though the practice of mission may give rise to a certain kind of theology, the latter will essentially be either a modification or development of the theology that motivated mission in the first place. To be aware of this fact is essential today in the sense that it is to be conscious of not only how mission is done, but of the forces that drive it. It is to try to understand what particular cultural experiences or conditionings embedded in theological conceptions influence missionary performances. These may easily blind the missionary from recognizing the value of different particularities other than their own and as a consequence preventing the realization of the ultimate goal of mission: the promotion of the "fraternal coexistence of all peoples" that Pope John Paul II speaks about.

The significance of a specific theological perspective for mission is not new. When Jesus commissioned the first disciples, he had a clear theological vision in mind. We can discern it from the various accounts of his life and teaching in the New Testament. Jesus' perspective of mission is summarized succinctly above all in the ultimate passage of the Gospel according to Matthew (28:19–20). From the beginning of the Christian movement, this passage has provided the basic reason for mission activity: "teach them to obey all that I have commanded you."

Very early on in the Church, the Apostle Peter expands on his earlier theological confession in Jesus, as "the Christ, the Son of the living God" (Matt 16:16), by uncompromisingly defending this foundational theology of mission. He does so first in his address to the people assembled in Jerusalem after the descent of the Holy Spirit upon the disciples to strengthen them (Acts

2:14–36), but definitively when he and the other disciples come under orders from the Jewish religious authorities to cease and desist from transmitting the message of Christ. The disciples' position cannot be clearer: "We must obey God rather than human beings!" (Acts 5:29).

Of course, it is clear from the Book of Acts and from the Epistles in general that from the very beginning, the practice of mission gave different and very significant slants to this basic conviction. This was necessary as different questions arose, arising from practical circumstances that Jesus had not had to confront in his lifetime in such a direct way. From the New Testament it is obvious that the most significant of these questions happened to be cultural: namely, what to do when non-Jews (uncircumcised or Gentile peoples) wished in good faith to become followers of Jesus and were willing to obey all that Jesus himself had commanded? Paul of Tarsus faced this extremely difficult mission question head-on and gave rise to the mission theology of cultural inclusiveness within the primitive Christian communities. By his bold translation of Jesus' original and enduring sense of mission as encompassing positive values from all cultures, Paul may be accredited, both sociologically and theologically, with the initiative of the outward expansion of the Church from the narrow Jewish cultural confines to universal mission. The practical catholicity of mission is a fruit of Paul's pioneering vision and initiative.

In response to Jesus' original imperative to mission, founders of Religious Congregations and Societies also tapped deeply into Paul's ingenuity to spread the Gospel beyond their own geographical and cultural confines. In Africa, for example, missionaries were immediately confronted by different cultural environments. They were constantly forced to answer different concrete questions resulting from these environments. This propelled the more perceptive among them to modify or even change their original theological perspectives, just as Paul had done.

On account of the complex relationship between theology in theory and its practice that gives rise to and defines approaches to mission, as Paul exemplifies in his ministry, it will be useful to take a quick look at how models of theology and the practice of mission have evolved in Africa since the beginning of the missionary enterprise. What were the first missionary visions of mission to Africa? What changes have occurred? How have the changes in turn necessitated new developments in the conception and practice of mission? What new models of mission have arisen?

Underlying the missionary activity of Paul is the conviction that human beings are products of their cultures and receive the Gospel message primarily as such. People are shaped by the physical as well as non-material environment in which they are born and raised. The latter include the thought forms, language, and symbols into which and by which they are socialized. Although these do not bind or determine people in an absolute way (and Paul seems to have understood this), they deeply shape how people perceive reality, themselves (their identity), their relationships to other people of the same culture, their perception of and relationship to people of different cultures from their own, and, very significantly, their perception of, and relationship with God. All of these processes are interrelated.

Since, as Pope John Paul II notes, the Gospel "transcends any human distinctions," Christian missionaries as ministers of the Gospel must to a certain extent transcend some particularities of their cultures to engage meaningfully in trans-cultural, intercultural, or cross-cultural dialogue and relationships. Indeed, this is the essence of the call to mission, as Paul realized. Yet since no one can completely disassociate oneself from one's culture, one will always remain visitors before the cultural other. Paul himself proudly declared more than once in a single episode that he was a Jew and that he was thoroughly versed in his Jewish culture and religion (Acts 21:39; 22:3). This indicates the complexity as well as the beauty of mission because, at its best, mission desires and allows the missionary to enter intimately into respectful contact with the culturally different other. A fuller understanding of God as the ultimate "Other" is in this way enhanced.

Genuine Christian mission is therefore always a two-way process; it involves the dynamics of giving and receiving. While the missionary cannot but offer the experience of the Gospel as received and interpreted by his or her own particular cultural meditation, he or she should be prepared to receive those genuine values by the grace of God already indwelling in every culture. These values contribute to the interpretation of the Gospel in a new way so that with both influences taken seriously into account—the "I" and the "Thou"—the understanding of the Gospel will often grow in a spiral-like fashion to ever higher dimensions.

It is useful to reiterate some historical paradigms of mission theology in Africa in order to see how they influenced the situation of vocations promotion to the religious life. Although the portraits as presented may look like caricatures, the results they prompted in terms of vocations advancement to religious life are essentially accurate. They may be categorized into three main theological patterns consecutively, in tandem with historical political events: Mission as salvation of the heathens; Mission as civilization; and Mission as dialogue.

At the very beginning of missionary work in Africa in the nineteenth century, the controlling missiological paradigm was the salvation of the heathens. It was a racist one, a hangover from the ideology of the period of the slave trade, when the nagging question was whether blacks were truly human, or their cultures equally endowed with the presence of God. During this era, mission was understood in an exclusively spatial sense. For Africa, it entailed Europeans leaving Europe to go save the "blighted souls" of Africans. In this view, Africans would forever be lost in hell on account of the biblical curse cast upon them (see Gen 9:21–25) unless they heard the Gospel. To this end, in 1873, Pope Pius IX attached a three-hundred-day indulgence to a prayer he composed and recommended to be said for divine mercy on the souls of the "poor" Africans. The prayer represents a perfect example of a pessimistic theological hypothesis concerning the African people in the divine plan of salvation. The Pope described Africans as spiritually, "the most wretched" on earth. According to the prayer, unless Africans are helped to discard "their idols" they would be condemned to remain perpetually in their existing condition of "darkness and the shadow of death." The introductory part of the prayer runs this way:

> Let us pray for the most wretched Ethiopians in Central Africa, that Almighty God may at length move the curse of Cham [Ham] from their hearts, and grant them the blessing to be found only in Jesus Christ, our God and Lord.[1]

And the famed British colonial administrator, Lord F. J. D. Lugard (1858–1945), one-time Governor General of Nigeria, had likewise no lack of choice phrases to describe Africa and the Africans along similar lines. He labeled Africa "the abode of barbarism and cruelty" and Africans as almost beastlike, without "self-control, discipline, and foresight." Lord Lugard was of the opinion that "through the ages the Africans appear to have evolved no organized religious creed, and though some tribes appear to believe in a deity, the religious sense seldom rises above pantheistic animalism and seems more often to take the form of a vague dread of the supernatural."[2]

These examples make it easy to see that with such fundamentally cynical theology about an entire race as foundation for mission, it was the exceptional Religious Institute which would advocate that African young women and men might be admitted to the ranks of the group as religious on an equal footing as anyone else. It is not that it did not happen; but it was rare and when it did, it was as a rule circumscribed by the most stringent conditions.

---

1. "Oremus et pro misteririmis Africae Centralis populis Aethiopum, ut Deus omnipotens tandem aliquando auferat maledictionem Chami a cordibus eorum, detque illis benedictionem, unice in Jesu Christo, Det et Domino nostro consequendam."

2. Lugard, *Dual Mandate in British Tropical Africa*, 70.

Closely associated with the theology of mission as salvation of heathens was the idea of mission as civilization. These approaches to mission touched more directly on the patterns of thought, values, and behavior of the African peoples. By this time, Europe had conceded that Africans also had cultures, but they were invariably characterized as "primitive," "savage," "barbaric," and "pagan." Like the colonial agenda, the missionary objective was generally to abolish them, to replace them with European values, and thereby "civilize" the people. This was the "white man's burden" that both colonial civil administrations and missionary Church authorities were convinced they had to carry.

The missionary objective was not to save the Africans through or within their cultures (as was the exceptional vision of some founders of Missionary Institutes). On the contrary, the strategy was, whenever possible, to save Africans outside their cultures. This was the transplantation method of mission. Missionaries identified western civilization and its particular interpretation of the Gospel with the Gospel of Christ itself, tolerating no alternative translation from the experience of Africa. For the transplantation approach, faith in Christ had to be expressed and lived in Africa exactly as in the West. It was a "take it-or-leave-it" package deal, complete with such concrete, environmentally and culturally understood liturgical signs and symbols like bread and wine. The answer was an *a priori* "no" to any attempt to understand Christian dogmas and ethical practices through African spiritual and religious eyes. Inculturation would have been then an unforgivable—or at least "reserved"—sin!

The dispensaries and schools that missionaries established everywhere they went were a good thing for the wrong reason because they were primarily intended as a means of "de-Afrizanization." Thus the catechetical process in many places in Africa was generally described in terms of "reading," equated with civilization. Reading underlined the importance of the written word over morality. The power which the spoken "word" held in the African oral tradition was thereby almost totally dismissed. Consequently, few, if any, Religious Communities thought of modifying their patterns of life to accommodate the deep-seated African psycho-social and cultural significance of the spoken word, including the associated values of personal presence, hospitality, general conviviality, a sense of social egalitarianism, and respect for elders and ancestors in the day-to-day life of their communities. One could even add that in some Congregations African foods and the manner of dress were similarly treated. Therefore, many African members of Religious Communities silently suffered a constant sense of frustration, distress, and resentment, sometimes leading to belligerent, despondent, and resentful behavior. But as St. Augustine warned, "resentment is like taking poison and hoping the other person dies."

Vatican II would, however, profoundly begin to change these views of mission on both the theoretical-theological and the practical-pastoral levels. The Conciliar documents *Ad Gentes*, *Nostra Aetate*, and *Dignitatis Humanae* were key to this revolution. In *Ad Gentes* (no. 13), the Council reverses what would have been standard practice in the previous models of mission, like "forcing anyone to embrace the faith, or alluring or enticing people by unworthy techniques." Since it was previously believed that non-Christian cultures did not have any trace of divine truth, it seemed only right that they be brought to it by any means necessary. On the contrary, *Dignitatis Humanae* (no. 10) turns this assumption completely on its head, stating bluntly that "in matters religious every manner of coercion . . . should be excluded," whether physical or psychological. The document establishes conscience and free will as the sole principles in religious conversion.

With regard to culture, *Ad Gentes* (no. 22) was equally radical and revolutionary. It urges local Churches "to borrow" anything "from the customs and traditions of their people, from their wisdom and their learning, from their arts and sciences" that can enhance the understanding of God and the message of Christ. By doing so, "it will be more clearly seen in what ways faith can seek for understanding in the philosophy and wisdom of these peoples. A better view will be gained of how their customs, outlook on life, and social order can be reconciled with the manner of living taught by divine revelation. As a result, avenues will be opened for a more profound adaptation in the whole area of Christian life." *Nostra Aetate* (no. 2) asserts the same thing.

From Vatican II and the two African synods so far, new models of mission inevitably follow. Their main characteristics include a commitment by the missionary to presence and to sincere and respectful conversation with Africa; collaboration in social ministry; and healing of persons in the sense of mercy and compassion. Just like the process of theology, the major components of these new models of mission involve two motifs relevant to the circumstances of the contemporary Church in Africa: Inculturation and Liberation.

As more and more Africans become members of international Religious Institutes, a serious question confronts them: How have or can the Institutes' charisms be interpreted in the social, economic, and political context of Africa? Concretely, what specific areas of social life and spirituality need to be cultivated, changed, or complemented, taking into account the mix of persons and cultures constituting membership of the particular Congregation or Society? As Pope John Paul II put it in *Redemptoris Missio* (no. 37), "the rapid and profound transformations which characterize today's world, especially in the southern hemisphere, are having a powerful effect on the overall missionary picture." One of these deep transformations should be the integration in Religious Institutes of useful cultural traditions once despised in Africa. Unlike only a few decades ago, when Religious Institutes and the Church as a whole operated theologically and pastorally on a mainly western cultural model, today more and more Africans want to be proud of their cultures and often resent it when these are summarily dismissed or denigrated. Lack of attention to these feelings is likely to harm individuals emotionally, cause unnecessary tension, and in the long run seriously destabilize a Religious Community.

While it is not desirable to water down in any way the values a particular Institute stands for, contextualization or inculturation of religious life in Africa is necessary in order to free African Religious psychologically and emotionally from emotional debilities. The time has come to share the riches of African culture to enhance the horizons of any Religious Institute that has as members a considerable number of Africans. Of course, unity is always of the essence of both the Church and Religious Communities. Yet care must always be taken not to interpret unity too narrowly as uniformity. Uniformity in the long run frustrates the psychological and spiritual growth of both the individual and the community. The principle articulated so many centuries ago, presumably by St. Augustine of Hippo, is still valid: "In essentials, unity, in non-essentials, liberty, in all things, charity."[3]

In intercultural religious living, the role of culture cannot be emphasized enough. Culture is not an abstract reality detached from people. Culture is intimately connected with individuals and societies and their environment. It is not possible to conceive of a person without culture. This is what Vatican II in *Gaudium et Spes* (no. 53) affirms when it notes that "'culture' stands for everything by which human beings refine and develop their various capacities of mind and body." It is only through culture, the Council says, that "the human person ... [can] reach true and authentic humanity."

The *United Nations Educational, Scientific and Cultural Organization (UNESCO)* asserted similarly in 1982 that "it is through culture that we discern values and make choices. It is through culture that human beings express themselves, become aware of themselves, recognize their incompleteness, question their own achievements, seek untiringly for new meanings and create works through which they transcend their limitations."[4] Konrad Raiser of the World Council of Churches (WCC) also observed that culture "is the second 'nature' of human beings in their social relationships" inasmuch as it "refers to

---

3. Berlis, Necessaries Unitas, in Dubiis Libertas, 2011.

4. UNESCO, *Mexico City Declaration on Cultural Policies, World Conference on Cultural Policies Mexico City, 26 July-6 August 1982*, accessed June 12, 2016. http://portal.unesco.org/culture/en/files/12762/11295421661mexico_en.pdf/mexico_en.pdf

the delicate fabric of habits, symbols, ... rules of behavior [and] moral values" by which life is ordered.[5] For the Lausanne Committee for World Evangelization's Consultation on Gospel and Culture in Willowbank, Bermuda (1978):

> Culture is an integrated system of beliefs (about God or reality or ultimate meaning), of values (about what is true, good, beautiful and normative), of customs (how to behave, relate to others, talk, pray, dress, work, play, trade, farm, eat, etc.) and of institutions which express those beliefs, values and customs ... which bind a society together and gives it a sense of identity, dignity, security, and continuity.[6]

If this is what culture is, and if the relationship between individuals and their cultures is so fundamental to their self-realization and identity of persons, then it is clearly perilous to bypass, ignore, or ridicule any culture in the process of living our Christian vocation. We can worship God in truth only as cultural beings. We can live in harmony with others in community only as cultural beings. Are not these the two pillars of religious life? If it is through culture that, in the words of UNESCO, human beings gain self-consciousness and develop, the maturity of an individual in terms of intellectual capacity (IQ), emotional stability, honesty, respect, sociability, sexual maturity, and so on, must be examined from the perspective of the subject's or subjects' culture. The evaluation of and decision about the suitability or otherwise of a candidate to religious life must be made and taken within that context by the Vocations Promoter. Unfortunately, very little serious study has been done in the context of Africa in the field of psychology and behavioral sciences to establish the cultural habits of the African. In general, what are used so far are western criteria under which African candidates to religious life are selected and to which they are made to conform and imitate.

The practice at one time in some parts of Africa was not to accept offspring from polygamous families to religious life or the priesthood. The parents' marital canonical irregularity seemed to affect negatively the aptitude of the children for religious life. The practice was apparently based on the assumption that the parents' "irregular marriage" would set a "bad example" and similarly affect the children even when the latter intended to choose a different style of life, namely, consecrated life in the Church. With time, however, this kind of supposition of "guilt by association" was questioned and the barrier was largely lifted. In the Old Testament, the prophets Jeremiah (31:29–30) and Ezekiel (18:2) do not approve of the proverb: "The parents

---

5. Quoted in Gallagher, *Clashing Symbols*, 154.
6. Gallagher, *Clashing Symbols*, 152.

have eaten sour grapes, and the children's teeth are set on edge." Instead, they insist that "whoever eats sour grapes, their own teeth will be set on edge." This was the position of Jesus himself, who affirmed on an even loftier level about the man born blind (John 9:3) that even in such irregular situations, God shows what God can do for us.

There are other challenging situations apart from the canonical irregularity of polygamy. They include concerns about the offspring of single parent homes, especially single mothers, but also, increasingly, single fathers. May these be baptized as infants or not? In different dioceses across the continent there are different pastoral practices. Some admit them to baptism unconditionally; others attach conditions to it, such as that only the first child may be baptized; and still others do not baptize them at all, waiting until they are of age to take their own decision. More specifically for our topic, if an adult young man or woman, child of a single mother or father, expresses the desire to join religious life, what should be done?

It would seem that if society and the Church have mostly moved beyond the discriminating position against children born of polygamous unions, the Church ought to show the lead in the case of children of single parents as well. It seems unjust, where this still happens, to exclude *de jure* or *de facto* these children from the religious vocation simply on account of the circumstances of their birth, circumstances in which they themselves played no role. Fr. Festo Mkenda, a Jesuit historian of Christianity, wonders if such reluctance lies in the "unfounded fear that, because of their being brought up by a single parent, such children automatically and of necessity lack something in their moral and psychological aptitude." Yet, for him, "this view undermines the formative work of God himself and his ability to transcend human limitations." More significantly, it "fails to take into account the African broad circle of relationships (the extended family), where a son or daughter of my sister could find a father figure all over the place, including from among maternal uncles." Fr. Mkenda continues to suggest that accepting these candidates would even be of service to theology and the Church. As he put it: "getting children from single parent homes into the priesthood and religious life might be the best way to ensure that experiential knowledge about such homes can inform religious life, spirituality and, more generally, theology," so that "a more agreeable understanding of single parent families will emerge within the Church and a better approach to their pastoral care be developed."[7]

An important caution is in order at this point. It concerns the motivation of vocations promotion on the part of certain Religious Institutes. There is worldwide awareness now about the crime of human trafficking. It serves

---

7. Personal communication between the author and Fr. Festo Mkenda, SJ in 2014.

no purpose to hide the fact that the economic poverty of Africa makes prospects of living and working in Europe very attractive indeed for many young African persons. As is well known now, many Africans risk and often lose their lives to get to Europe in search of greener pastures. Religious Institutes must be extremely careful in vocation promotion to avoid giving this impression or remotely using people for reasons apart from pure dedication to God. Anything akin to human trafficking must be shunned, however innocuous it may seem on the surface.

Finally, one cannot overlook the fact that there are some negative dimensions within African culture as well whose effect is to diminish rather than enhance the humanity (*Ubuntu*) of the human person. One such is the reality of tribalism or negative ethnicity. Religious are not immune to this vice; they need to confront it directly in the candidates to and members of Religious Institutes. Just like the disease of racism, unwitting tribalism can be transposed into the life and functioning of Religious Communities, making them dysfunctional. Liberation from racism and negative ethnicity formed part of the vision of Vatican II and the two African synods. The effort should continue.

What qualities, then, should be sought in those young African people wishing to lead a religious life? There are some transcultural constants which should not be compromised for the religious vocation and transcultural living. These include

a. the ability to integrate faith and life based on the African conviction of the sacredness of all creation,

b. the ability to bond with others on a wide scale, something that should be instilled in the process of formation as a "rite of passage"; and

c. openness to ongoing dialogue with both tradition, based on the African value of respect for elders and change, sensitive to changing times.

Chapter 8

Dialogue with African Religion

JUDGING BY HOW FREQUENTLY it has been used in recent years in the areas of politics, international relations, and religion, the notion of dialogue appears to express a serious concern of the age. Yet it is by no means employed unambiguously; it carries different implications and in different contexts it suggests various levels of meaning for different users.[1]

"Dialogue" as a concept can be used to describe the most trivial of encounters as well as engagements of the utmost consequence for human and universal survival. For instance, the term is employed in the context of casual conversation, but also in reference to negotiations to end hostilities between and among nations, to foster reconciliation and justice in situations of conflict, preserve the ecology in environmental issues, or encourage mutual understanding among different faiths and religions. With so many contexts and forms, dialogue is not an easy notion to unpack. Therefore, it is important to establish its true meaning, especially as it is used in the religious sphere. In this setting, we may speak of several levels of, or approaches to, dialogue.

In 1991, the Vatican Pontifical Council for Interreligious Dialogue identified four useful approaches in its document, "Dialogue and Proclamation" (DP).[2] Although the document's interest is mainly with dialogue between the Christian religion (specifically Catholicism) and those typically described as

---

1. See also Magesa, *African Religion in the Dialogue*.

2. Pontifical Council for Interreligious Dialogue, "Dialogue and Proclamation: Reflections and Orientations on Interreligious Dialogue and Proclamation of the Gospel of Jesus Christ," accessed March 3, 2016. http://www.shinmeizan.com/images/PDF/DialProc-en.pdf.

"world religions," it applies to the process with African Religion as well. DP distinguishes between:

> (a) The dialogue of life, where people strive to live in an open and neighbourly spirit, sharing their joys and sorrows, their human problems and preoccupations; (b) The dialogue of action, in which . . . [members of different faiths and religions] collaborate for the integral development and liberation of people; (c) The dialogue of theological exchange, where specialists seek to deepen their understanding of their respective religious heritages, and to appreciate each other's spiritual values; (d) The dialogue of religious experience, where persons, rooted in their own religious traditions, share their spiritual riches, for instance with regard to prayer and contemplation, faith and ways of searching for God or the Absolute (no. 42).

Despite the general theoretical agreement that all of these approaches are valid, their practical application is again different with different people and in different contexts. The emphasis might differ with each approach according to different faith communities. In fact, among the approaches, some may be rejected completely as objectionable or impractical in the framework of this faith community or the other. This would be the case, for example, with a faith-stance that disallows any reflection on the truth claims of its creed and dogmas, considering any such attempt as undermining accepted belief and the *raison d'etre* of the faith-community itself. The phenomenon known today as religious fundamentalism arises from this kind of position. Ultimately, a standpoint like this precludes any of the other approaches to dialogue, and so prevents any possibility of engaging in it. Consequently, religions remain completely isolated from and antagonistic towards one another. This was generally the predominant intellectual and institutional situation of relationships among religions prior to the 1960s.

However, since the last half of the twentieth century, there has been a change in the Churches and religious academic world which has enabled a new understanding and practice of dialogue and rendered interreligious dialogue generally desirable. The most central objective of dialogue in this new perception is to find and communicate meaning and, hopefully, shared meaning. David Lochhead describes dialogue correctly as "a search for understanding" rather than "agreement." Agreement or "common ground" may, of course, come about, and this would be a very welcome thing, "a gift of grace, an added bonus," but that is not the primary purpose of the process. The proper attitude in the practice of dialogue is this: "I will seek [only] to understand and to allow myself to be understood."³ Dialogue is demanding and is often avoided because it requires the full recognition of the identity of the other, a degree of self-exposure and, consequently, a measure of vulnerability. Honesty and transparency are ultimately the basis of true dialogue.

Interreligious dialogue can happen in either of two contexts: in situations of divergent philosophical convictions or spiritual worldviews, on the one hand or, on the other, within the framework of similar views and positions. The goal of authentic dialogue in either case should be, once again, the search for and sharing of meaning. Where there is conflict of views and convictions, the aim should be to seek access to the meaning of the other, whether or not this ends up in mutual agreement. As a goal, the process only calls for acceptance of the possibility of truth in the opposite position. Without this *a priori* intellectual stance in relations among faiths and religions, there cannot be true interreligious dialogue. In those instances where people share more or less similar convictions and views, dialogue entails the (desirable) possibility of deepening one's vision through that of the other. In the Christian context, this conversation is generally referred to as "ecumenism." Although all Christians share the same faith in Jesus, as well as the conviction that he is the Savior of the world, they still need to engage in conversation about this belief, because there are historical differences in its practical expression in terms of doctrine and ritual among denominations. But the deeper purpose is to obtain continually greater mutual appreciation as each denomination searches for a more profound sense of the meaning and mission of Jesus.

Since religious belief is based on the acceptance of the reality of Ultimate Meaning, therefore in the interreligious context dialogue is ultimately a search for the meaning of Meaning. It is at the same time a constant struggle for ways to express this Ultimate Meaning in real life. It is thus both a theoretical and practical endeavor involving the human mind and actual attitudes. What this means is that whoever is engaged in the dialogical process must try to discover the sense and practical implications of God's self-communication to the world within religious traditions using any, some, or all the mentioned approaches, and perhaps others. Eventually, this implies a search for authentic humanity as God reveals it in various cultural and religious traditions. According to Gordon W. Allport, citing Eduard Spranger, it is this effort that constitutes the "religious intention" or, indeed, "the sum of all religious intentions." The effort "represents a desire for total harmony [with the Divine], the individual's successive efforts to complete the incomplete, to perfect the imperfect, to conserve all values, eliminate all disvalues, to find permanence in the place of transitoriness."[4]

3. Lochhead, *Dialogical Imperative*, 64.
4. Allport, *Individual and His Religion*, 132.

This insight refers to the hypothesis that the value of authentic dialogue between and among religions "can be found only in the mystical goal of oneness."[5] This goal, though not sought as the *a priori* visible objective of the dialogical practice, is nonetheless assumed: there is a unity of humanity that our present, everyday experience does not, and cannot, fully reflect. Again, this premise is at the basis of all religious belief. Thomas E. Helm, following Rudolph Otto, perhaps explains the assumption best when he describes "mystery," from which the adjective "mystical" derives, as "the experience of awe and wonder associated with the divine or numinous presence of the divine."[6] Although this is something in creation and the human reality that the mind cannot fully grasp, a deep and sincere dialogical process sometimes leads people to break out of their ordinary isolations and in their rapprochement to encounter "the numinous presence of the divine" which is the source of human unity.

The search for "the mystical goal of oneness" is complex and must not be invoked in a reductionist manner as being capable of answering all questions and problems of relationships. Consequently, dialogue is not a mechanical solution to conflict. Rather it is basically a way towards greater truth and mutual understanding. It is first and foremost an attitude. Dialogue by itself does not bring about conciliation; it only facilitates the development towards it. More than anything, dialogue is ultimately a uniquely spiritual endeavor. Rather like the soul's longing for God who is Oneness par excellence, dialogue constitutes "a direction rather than an object." It is a movement towards, not a complete grasp of the divine Truth, which is God. Not to appreciate this point in the process of dialogue can seriously impede it. It can frustrate the dialogical partners and end up causing more mistrust than helping to promote the exploration for openness and mutual appreciation.

As a quest for mystical unity, authentic interreligious dialogue must by definition be voluntary. No dialogue can take place unless the partners in dialogue have freely chosen to engage in it, to listen to one another respectfully and learn even from the other's mistakes and fallacies. Dialogue cannot take place unless the process helps the partners to simultaneously enhance their own self-understanding and identity and that of their interlocutor's philosophical or spiritual convictions, acknowledging that no one can claim a monopoly of truth, especially in matters to do with Ultimate Truth. Dialogue thus acts like a ready mirror, reflecting the image of the dialogical partners to oneself and to each other. In dialogue, even silence is speech. Where one party does not or cannot articulate clearly the foundations of its beliefs, the other must listen to

---

5. Allport, *Individual and His Religion*, 4.
6. Helm, *Christian Religion*, 5.

the deeper heartbeat of its practices. What value for humanity do these practices carry? All participants in dialogue must themselves be ready to honestly examine their own images, projected by the other. If they are not intellectually and emotionally prepared to do so, or once free will is absent and coercion of any kind enters into the process, true dialogue ceases to exist. Whatever apparent positive results from an encounter of this kind, they will only be superficial and short-lived. True dialogue does not tolerate pretence.

The dialogical route often takes a long time, and may produce little or no immediate, conspicuous results; patience is an indispensable quality of genuine dialogue. It is not realistic to expect that convictions formed over a lifetime, will be transformed within a short-term encounter. But any and every step towards mutual understanding is a positive note in the inner and more important dialogical symphony, even when the instruments appear disparate. What is primary is the interior state of the dialogue partners because it forms the condition for the external and, hopefully, more permanent transformation. Both sides are obviously intimately connected, yet it should be evident that to concentrate on external change with little interior conversion of spirit, perception and attitudes is a failure on a crucial point of the dialogical process.

Moreover, dialogue is not a linear development; in their psyche and moral behavior, human beings do not consistently proceed forward. There are often curves, valleys and hills and even reversals and backtracking in the journey. This is why dialogue may be qualified quite justifiably as an unending process: some tensions may never be completely overcome. Nevertheless, one hopes that at every moment of the encounter, sincere partners in dialogue will build upon any positive step previously achieved and continually strengthen a sense of common trust. Might we call this an adventure in attaining an ever-expanding horizon? In case of regression to previous attitudes and behavior, the process of dialogue, if authentic, can never be abandoned. Partners in dialogue must be ready to undergo what can be a painful process of starting again and again, each time even almost from the beginning. But they must do so every time with new determination to create a fresh situation of goodwill and trust.

These conditions for dialogue are important to contextualize this discussion concerning dialogue between Christian and African religious traditions. The need for conversation between them should not be a subject of debate any longer as it was until the 1960s. For a number of reasons, dialogue is now imperative.

The idea that African spirituality and religious practices would disappear with time under the influence of Christianity and western education has been proved wrong. African spirituality remains alive and active and often clashes with western Christian positions and expectations. Instead of merely ridiculing African living spirituality, as was the case for a long time, the Christian tradition must enter into serious conversation with it, because it forms the basis of the worldview of millions of people not only in Africa but worldwide.

The relative political, economic and social isolation that distinguished the African continent from the rest of the world only a century ago is no longer the case. Africa has become an important global player in every respect. In the contemporary world, adherents of African Religion, likewise, cannot avoid contact with other religious traditions. Moreover, African religionists are no longer ashamed of their spirituality as an "inferior" religious orientation. On the contrary, they are progressively recovering, appropriating, and representing their own spiritual roots and identity with pride. Adherents of African Religion realize the need to engage in inter-religious dialogue for the sake of their own human and religious maturity. The phenomenon of the African Initiated Churches (AICs) all across the continent testifies to this widespread process. Though often not well articulated as dialogue of theological exchange, the interpenetration of Christian and African religious elements in AICs is quite evident. It incorporates the four forms of dialogue at different degrees.

Peace and reconciliation constitute a third factor that makes dialogue between African Religion and Christianity imperative. What thinkers like Hans Küng, Paul Knitter, Stephen Neill, John Cobb, and John Hick have said about the necessity of dialogue among religions in the interests of world peace applies equally here. Since the encounter between Christianity and African Religion has historically not promoted mutual appreciation, with Christianity tending to suppress African spirituality through psychological or even at times actual physical forms of pressure, mistrust has been the result. This has done more harm than good to the development of peace in Africa.

An issue that is sometimes raised and that must be addressed is whether dialogue between Christianity and African Religion is possible at all. Since the two faith traditions are at many points so different in theology and structure, some observers argue that dialogue between them is a practical impossibility; it cannot even start. They contend that these religious worldviews are like language structures; each has its own underlying tone and the two cannot be harmonized. The claim is, consequently, that Christianity and African Religion are at best condemned to lead parallel existences by logic of their inner nature. Each must live in its own world. The only options foreseeable in the encounter between African Religion and Christianity, according to this opinion, include mutual indifference, perpetual conflict, or domination of one over the other.

This line of thinking succumbs to the misconception of the meaning of interreligious dialogue that we have discussed since it misconstrues the goal of dialogue to be agreement rather than mutual understanding. From our analysis of the meaning and goal of true dialogue, a sincere attempt to understand and appreciate differences between the African and Christian concepts of God, for instance, would itself be the privileged moment in the dialogical encounter between them, because it would lead both towards a glimpse of the mystery of human unity in God beneath the differences. Without necessarily achieving it concretely, this is what we seek in the first place as the heart of dialogue. It ultimately constitutes the essence of possible intellectual, spiritual and attitudinal transformation. With this starting point, even particular "non-negotiables" can benefit from the encounter. Basic convictions and positions in individuals may not appear to change drastically, but if deeper self-appreciation of each tradition takes place, interreligious dialogue will have achieved its primary purpose.

Moreover, from historical and contemporary evidence, the reciprocal exclusivity of language structures that some have alluded to is contestable and ultimately unsustainable. Upon encountering another language over a period of time, it may indeed still retain its essential structure. However, when different languages mingle through use by the same group of people in a given locality for a considerable time, they are often modified, sometimes drastically, by borrowing expressions from one another or adjusting their grammar. This happens especially when new facts previously unknown in the world of one language are introduced into its space by another. Many African languages, while retaining their grammatical and syntactic distinctiveness, have borrowed extensively from the colonial languages of English, French, or Portuguese and thus changed significantly. As in the case of a number of creolized languages, of which there are several in Africa, linguistic encounter may result in a new form of language altogether. Pidgin English in parts of West Africa is an example. Kiswahili in East Africa was born partially as a result of intermarriage between Arabic and local coastal languages of the region. The birth of a new language out of a combination of two or several is even stronger proof of the success of spontaneous dialogical processes in relation to verbal communication. There are examples of a similar process in the Christian and African religious encounter.

Apart from the negative aspects involved in the encounter between Christianity and African Religion that the history of Christianity records, where the paradigm was coercion and suppression of indigenous cultures or indifference towards them, there are also numerous instances of genuine contextualization. In the latter case, it was mostly an intuitive and practical process, responding to real questions that people were facing in their belief and worship systems. It may be referred to as "popular inculturation." The academic, doctrinal, official level only followed this, to offer needed clarifications where tensions between different beliefs and practices occurred: What linguistic expressions and symbols could be accepted as expressions of Christian belief ? Were the current Gnostic representations of God suitable? Could all Roman imperial symbols of power be incorporated in the organization of the Church, and if not on what basis should the selection be made and how?

The encounter between Christianity and African Religion was driven by the Christian imperative to evangelize. Whereas African Religion was and has remained a non-proselytizing religion, content to have its adherents born into it, Christianity was from the start an innately missionary movement. Its first devotees took the mandate to "go and make disciples of all nations" (see Matt 28:19, Acts 2:38, Mark 16:15) seriously as the mark that distinguished them from Judaism. Taking advantage of the relative peace created by the Roman Empire and Greco-Roman culture, Christianity spread to North Africa, Egypt and Ethiopia already by the late first or early second century. According to legend, some of the very first disciples of Jesus evangelized in Egypt (Mark) and Ethiopia (Matthew).

Although administratively Roman, these regions are geographically African and were at the time also demographically so. Greco-Roman cultures existed there alongside the African. Although carried in these parts by Greek and Roman linguistic systems, Christianity nevertheless inevitably absorbed many of the existing cultural realities to produce a unique expression of the Christian faith, distinct from the Palestinian kind. This also applied to Christian literature emanating from this region. In Alexandria in Egypt, there was a large presence of Greek-speaking Jews known as the Hellenists, so that before the dawn of the Christian Era, the oldest translation of the Hebrew Bible into Greek, the Septuagint (LXX), was made here for Hellenists. Conceivably, its Greek expressions spoken at the time in Alexandria by Hellenized Jews incorporated local cultural elements.

Historian Elizabeth Isichei notes the generally acknowledged fact that, "in the first Christian centuries, northern Africa provided some of the keenest intellects and most influential apologists in Christendom." We find them in the persons of Origen, Tertullian, and Augustine, among others, who were natives of Alexandria (in Egypt), Carthage (in modern Tunisia), and Thagaste (in modern Algeria) respectively. Philosophies and movements originating from this region, as for example, Gnosticism and Donatism, grappled with basic faith issues that still engage worldwide Christianity today, including the very meaning of Jesus, the nature and purpose of evil in the divine economy, and the sense of salvation itself. As Isichei notes, "at the end of the 3rd century AD, the eastern Maghreb [modern day Morocco, Algeria, Tunisia and Libya] was one of perhaps three places in the world where Christians were in a majority," other than Armenia and modern Turkey.[7] This is something that can justifiably be described as an "African Christianity." Its contemporary evidence is Coptic Christianity in Egypt and Ethiopia. The first phase of Christianity in Africa, from the late first to the sixth century, therefore, did not experience the negative complexes towards non-European contexts and cultures that later developed during its inculturation in Europe that were transposed into sub-Saharan Africa during the third and ongoing phase of the evangelization of the continent since the late nineteenth century.

During the second phase of Christianity in Africa, which corresponds with the era of the European trade in African slaves from about the fifteenth up to the early nineteenth century, there was not any attempt at meaningful encounter between African and Christian spiritual beliefs. "Christianity was brought to Africans bearing slavery and a discriminatory baggage," laments Maillu.

> Was it the black skin that devalued the black . . . [person] from full humanness to justify the white man's extraordinary and abominable enslaving of a creature he thought looked sub-human. Indeed, at that time, the African was valued above all as "a precious commodity"; African religious beliefs only served to prove the black people's sub-humanity to the slave traders and, in the eyes of their "Christian" Church. It is not surprising, then, that given this stance towards the African peoples, Christianity disappeared from the scene with the end of the slave trade.[8]

After about four centuries, Christianity again entered the sub-Saharan region of Africa, this time closely associated with the European colonial and imperial movements, thereby also carrying most of their negative baggage towards the African continent and its peoples. The colonial enterprise was only slightly distinguishable in African eyes from the trade in slaves in that it was more interested in raw materials that Africa could supply. Yet its attitude was not much different from slave times. For the colonialists and most Christian missionaries of the nineteenth and the first half of the twentieth centuries, the primary goal was to "civilize the natives." This meant to change Africans as completely as possible from their mental and spiritual outlook

---

7. Isichei, *History of Christianity*, 1–2.
8. Maillu, "Trying to Understand One Another," 2011.

into the European one. The violence perpetrated against African Religion in the process is not hard to imagine.

Even if, as George Kocholickal advises, Africans must "move beyond the period of 'lamentation' (about the evils committed against . . . [African Religion]) to the period of reconstruction where the goal is a more positive one of understanding African Religion's contribution to Africa itself and humanity,"[9] the historical experience of the encounter between African Religion and Christianity must still be kept in the foreground of the discussion. Despite the lessons about inculturation and liberation that African theology is trying to inculcate, it is important to keep the historical memory alive. Only then can the fire of reconstruction keep burning in Africa. African Religion must keep struggling for self-identity and Christianity for perseverance in the new perception of mission in line with the spirit of openness unveiled by Vatican II in the Catholic Church as well as in many denominations since the second half of the twentieth century.

Although many Christian denominations have publicly acknowledged the mistake in their previous methods of evangelization and endorsed a change in these methods, it does not mean that transformation in thought and attitudes has sufficiently come about. There are still many instances of hesitation and backsliding. A hopeful statement may be made, but its practical implementation may cause more questions than it was meant to answer. Adherents of African Religion sometimes become cynical because of the negative experiences they suffer at the hands of Christianity with its advantageous position in structures and public relations, and almost give up hope of ever having their identities respected. This situation can only be amended through an honest, but not rancorous, acknowledgement of the facts of history by both sides. Apart from this, it will be difficult for holistic reconstruction to happen as a result of dialogue.

Having insisted on the fact that the goal of dialogue is not necessarily agreement but mutual understanding, it is nevertheless always wise to begin any dialogue with those areas that hold the greatest possibility of agreement in mind. However disparate the worldviews, cultures or particular perspectives, it is highly unlikely that there will be no such points of contact, and therefore of positive communication, among people. What is necessary is that the attitudes on all sides in the conversation are positively oriented in the direction towards mystical oneness. With goodwill and respect for one another that are the fundamental requirements of true dialogue, a few such points will surface, resulting in spiritual enrichment for all. This fact is being recognized by many but the most fundamentalist of religionists. Of course, there are some

9. Kocholickal, "Interreligious Dialogue as a Form of Mission," 2011.

individuals and groups who will not accept this premise, but the result of this myopic position and closed-mindedness is extremely destructive.

Most new Pentecostal movements originating from the United States and the Korean peninsula exemplify this fundamentalist view in Africa. They sport the replacement approach which seeks to eradicate African spirituality altogether and to put in its stead a completely new "Christian" one. The model equates the necessarily limited and partial western experience of the faith with the total understanding of Christ. However, once again, no one culture or cluster of cultures can capture the latter. Complete comprehension of the mystery of Christ can only be an eschatological experience. Ultimately, therefore, on account of the cultural nature of religious experience and expression, the replacement model is culturally imperialistic and reductionist. It pushes a transplantation form of the faith that never succeeds in sending deep roots in the host culture.

There are two patterns of discourse between African Religion and Christianity that are feasible: the fulfillment and transcendence models. Both have their basis in the Scriptures and ultimately coalesce into one, the Christological model or "the human-face-of-God model." It is founded on the theology of the Incarnation which, in turn, at least in African theology, is the basis and justification for inculturation.

By his Incarnation, Jesus sanctified humanity only by receiving a human body. In doing so, Jesus became to the world "the human face of God." By the Incarnation, humanity could now recognize its authentic self, its divine possibility, and eventual fulfillment through Jesus because of this dynamics of the divine-human exchange of gifts. The human aspect in the dynamics is by no means less significant: Jesus saved the world through his humanity as much as through his Divinity. Inculturation theology takes this point seriously. Salvation implies a two-way street, the dynamics of giving and receiving.

The fundamental perception of inculturation theology is the same. When the Christian faith arrives in a place and culture, it receives just about as much as it gives. It renders cultural distinctions and prejudices irrelevant. All cultures are God's and from them God calls forth sons and daughters through faith. The message and practice of Christ's Gospel are geared towards fulfillment of culture and humanity, not their destruction. But it is fulfillment on two sides: on the part of African Religion on account of the glimpse into the reality of Jesus Christ that the Scriptures and Christians practice offer, and on the part of Christianity (as currently expressed), possibly a better view and understanding of the imperatives of the Gospel through the divine revelation already present in the new culture. There is spiritual value, incomplete though it might be, existing *a priori* in each of the two realities. A proper encounter between them through genuine, authentic, or true dialogue, creates a new reality, transcending each and both of them.

The goal of dialogue is reciprocal complementarity. Peter Phan argues that "This reciprocity in no way endangers the faith confession that the [Christian] Church has received from Christ, the fullness of revelation" because "it is one thing to receive a perfect and unsurpassable gift, and quite another to understand it fully and to live it completely." According to Phan, "It is therefore only in dialogue with other religions that Christianity can come to a fuller realization of its own identity and mission and a better understanding of the unique revelation that it has received from Christ, and vice versa, other religions can achieve their full potential only in dialogue with each other and with Christianity."[10]

This is what conversion should mean, not as replacing one worldview by another, but in the sense of "enlarging spiritual consciousness," specifically, becoming a new person in Christ, ever freshly understood. We find here the Christian "significance of things." Through dialogue, we come closer to Christ, who is "the whole" meaning, "the last word." "But this meaning is never understood, this last word is never spoken; always they remain superior, the ultimate meaning being a secret which reveals itself repeatedly, only nevertheless to remain eternally concealed. It implies an advance to the farthest boundary, where only one sole fact is understood: that all comprehension is 'beyond.'"[11]

Transcendence challenges all the old ways and beckons everyone to grow into a new understanding of Jesus Christ. But this sense of transcendence implies an ongoing task. Having grown into the new personhood or transcended the old ways, the task of examining the new world's competence vis-à-vis Gospel demands begins immediately, invigorated by values gleaned from the previous understandings. This procedure is similar to that of the hermeneutic or pastoral circle or spiral advocated by the theologians of liberation or, again, the See-Judge-Act triangular method of the Young Christian Workers. Fulfillment or transcendence in this model must continue to grow from one level to another until it finds complete eschatological fulfillment in Christ.

However, the approach to dialogue advocated here does not imply nonbelongingness. Belonging is a prerequisite for being human. The social group to which I belong and in which I participate forms me; it makes me what I am. I participate in it because I share in its values. So, even when I transcend my present beliefs in the sense of fulfilling them, I do so within the milieu of my identity as a Christian and an African. I fully belong to both identities as they gradually coalesce into one. The celebration of the sacraments should testify

10. Phan, *Being Religious Interreligiously*, 502.
11. Hyers, "Rethinking the Doctrine," 171–88.

to my new identity by not duplicating rituals but by combining values from both into a new ritual; similarly with other areas of belief and practice. This is what is described as the desire to be "at the same time truly Christian and truly African." Pope Paul VI thought in the same way. "If you are able to avoid the . . . danger of making your Christian profession into a kind of local folklore, or into exclusivist racism, or into egoistic tribalism or arbitrary separatism," he advised the Christians of Africa, "then you will be able to remain sincerely African even in your own interpretation of the Christian life; you will be able to formulate Catholicism in terms congenial to your own culture; you will be capable of bringing to the Catholic Church the precious and original contribution of 'negritude', which she needs particularly in this historic hour."[12]

Christianity will not take deep root in Africa unless it takes African Religion and spirituality as serious conversation partners at all levels. For its part, African spirituality must also take the dialogue between itself and Christianity seriously if it is to transcend its limited self, and find new values in both itself and Christianity that have hitherto been hidden or perceived only vaguely, as through a misty glass. To have an "African Christianity" requires a listening ear from African spirituality. The latter "should not refuse, but rather eagerly desire, to draw, from the patrimony of the patristic, exegetical, and theological tradition of the . . . Church, those treasures of wisdom which can rightly be considered universal, above all, those which can be most easily assimilated by the African mind."[13]

---

12. Paul VI, "Eucharistic Celebration at the Conclusion of the Symposium Organized by the Bishops of Africa: Homily of Paul VI, Kampala (Uganda), 31 July 1969."

13 Paul VI, "Eucharistic Celebration," 12.

Chapter 9

New Approaches to Mission

When you speak to a person in a language that he understands, it goes to his head. When you speak to him in his own language, it goes to his heart.

—Nelson Mandela

If I preach the Gospel, this is no reason for me to boast for an obligation has been imposed on me, and woe to me if I do not preach it! . . . Although I am free in regard to all, I have made myself a slave to all so as to win over as many as possible. To the Jews I became like a Jew to win over Jews; to those under the law I became like one under the law—though I myself am not under the law—to win over those under the law. To those outside the law I became like one outside the law—though I am not outside God's law but within the law of Christ—to win over those outside the law. To the weak I became weak, to win over the weak. I have become all things to all, to save at least some. All this I do for the sake of the Gospel, so that I too may have a share in it (1 Cor 19:16–23).

According to Pope Paul VI's Apostolic Exhortation *Evangelii Nuntiandi*, three fundamental factors constitute the nature and mission of the Church in the world. They pertain to the content, context, and method of transmission of the faith. These factors seek to address specific questions in the life of the Church. What do we believe about and what do we understand to be the origin, source and ultimate goal of our belief? In other words, to whom does the Church owe ultimate fidelity? This question concerns the content of the Catholic faith. Secondly, what circumstances inform our practical belief on a daily basis today? Here arises the issue of the context or environment in which the faith has to be concretely lived. Finally, how must we hand over to others the gift of faith in Jesus as Savior of the world? This concerns the way to transmit the faith from generation to generation. Since the beginning, the Church has understood itself to be called to these obligations and has defined its very existence in terms of their goal.[1]

These are questions that touch upon the very core of the meaning and purpose of the Church's existence. As part and parcel of the Church's life, they continue to engage it, and will do so for as long as she endures. It is possible to compress these issues without doing too much violence to them into two major discussion points. One has to do with the "shape" of the Church, or "what catholicity has meant inside the Church." The other concerns the Church's intrinsic call to mission, or "how the Church sees its purpose in and for the world, and ... understands evangelization" as her reason for existence."[2]

From a missiological perspective, considering events that took place within the Church as a guide, the major factors influencing the Church's own self-perception in Africa has been constituted by the long epoch influenced by the decisions of the Council of Trent, the period immediately after the Second Vatican Council, and the time of the general and particular synods in the Church since the end of Vatican II.

Since the Council of Trent (1545–63), the Catholic Church was galvanized under the single motivation of countering heresy and protecting the integrity of the Institutional Church thought to have been tarnished by the Protestant Reformation. Trent was a Dogmatic Council and so the defense of the conceptual teaching of the Church was its main preoccupation. Trent's mood was overwhelmingly inward-looking and defensive, and characterized all of post-Tridentine Church self-perceptions throughout the world. Paradoxically, this period also saw the phenomenal expansion of the Church all over the globe. Therefore, much of Catholic mission outlook was formed "at the most rigid, the most neo-scholastic, the most ultramontane, the most centralized half-century in the history of Catholicism—that is to say 1870–1920."[3] The Church saw itself as completely homogenous, describing its nature as

---

1. For an exhaustive discussion on new approaches to mission, relevant also to Africa, see Bosch, *Transforming Mission*, 1991.

2. Schreiter, *New Catholicity*, 122.

3. See Schreiter, *New Catholicity*, 122–27.

"one, Roman, Catholic, and Apostolic," with perhaps an exaggerated emphasis on "Roman" as a result of the definition on papal infallibility of the First Vatican Council (1869–70).

Pope John XXIII sensed the oddity of this self-perception of the Church and acted to renew it "in such a revolutionary way" that the change was "irreversible." He did so by convoking the Second Vatican Council with the aim of bringing the Church more in line with the image of Jesus in the New Testament, the Good Shepherd. Unlike Trent and Vatican I, Vatican II was therefore a Pastoral Council, less inward-looking, more attuned to the world and its surroundings. In a sense, the Pope wanted to open up sincere dialogue between the Church and the world. He was not afraid to do this for he saw the Church "as a garden to be tended, not a museum of antiques." Thus he defined his Pontifical program in a speech on January 25, 1959 in terms of *aggiornamento*. He wanted to modernize the Church, to bring it up to date, to make it take more seriously, than had been the case, what was happening in the world as the reason for her existence. But this was a shock to many, accustomed as they were to the Church as unchangeable, to the certainties of Trent and Vatican I. On his death bed, a cardinal is reported to have lamented in this way about Pope John XXIII: "Fifty years will be needed to repair the damage he has done to the Church in the five years of his pontificate."[4] However, what the cardinal saw as the "damage" to the Church has resisted repair fifty years on. On the contrary, it seems to offer the most plausible basis of defining the nature and activity of the Church as time passes.

If Pope John XXIII's vision for Vatican II has not been realized in its full and radical expressions, there has nevertheless been enough change of perspective in the Church because of it to warrant talk of a new period for the Church. For example, it is possible to speak of a movement for the "democratization" of the Church after the manner of the early Church before the rise of the hierarchical episcopate. Here, all members of the Church had a voice whereby they could exercise their priestly ministry received through baptism. A recent striking example of this was Pope John Paul II's call for an open, universal discussion on the exercise of the Petrine Ministry, something that would have been unthinkable during the period preceding Vatican II. Again, it might be debatable to what extent the theological vision of Vatican II, with its emphasis on dialogue, collegiality, communion, and service within the Church and between the Church and the world has influenced the pastoral practice of the Church. Nevertheless, the Council was the beginning of significant shifts in the theology and pastoral practice of the Church. The institution of the synods exemplifies this.

4. Rendina, *The Popes*, 594–96.

Of singular interest have been the particular or special synods, convened to address issues facing a given local Church. Almost every continent (and a few countries, such as The Netherlands and Lebanon) has had one or two such synods dedicated to it. Africa has had two special assemblies, in 1994 and 2009. Both addressed pressing issues from which the Church cannot turn away: the occasional specter of the genocide in various African countries, massive corruption and civil strife in many others. The work of the synods so far has sprung from the realization that God saves the world through the structures of human society, through the daily activities of women and men in the world.

Taking the two special synods on Africa, this is clearly what is being attempted. Inculturation featured prominently as a central theme of the First Synod because of the rise of awareness of the importance of African culture in authentic evangelization if faith is to be integrated with life, with the "deep structure" of African thought. The gap that exists between the dominant expressions of faith in Christ clothed mainly in western cultural language and the African spiritual worldview creates a kind of double religious existence among African Christians. This must be overcome. The Second Synod's emphasis on justice, reconciliation and peace captured the yearning of the African poor, oppressed not only internally by corrupt leaders, but also externally by international structures of injustice, to be free. True Christian faith cannot exist without justice or human communion happen without peace. Proposition 14 for the second African synod spelled this out:

> . . . the fruit of reconciliation between God and humanity, and within the human family itself, is the restoration of justice and the just demands of relationships. This is because God justifies the sinner by overlooking his or her sins, or one justifies an offender by pardoning his or her faults. And because God has justified us by forgiving our sins, so as to reconcile us to himself, we too can work out just relationships and structures among ourselves and in our societies, through pardoning and overlooking peoples' faults out of love and mercy. How else can we live in community and communion?[5]

The special synodal assemblies to date, whether national or continental, have attempted to avoid providing grand stories for the universal Church. And if there were universal answers proposed, they arose from concrete experiences of a given local Church. The Special Assembly for Asia in 1998

---

5. See La Santa Sede," Synodus Episcoporum: Ii Coetus Specialis Pro Africa, accessed July 21, 2016, http://www.vatican.va/roman_curia/synod/documents/rc_synod_doc_20091023_elenco-prop-finali_en.html

is a case in point. On account of the plurality, diversity, and strength of the Asian religions, and the very small presence of Christianity in that continent, it was important to address and highlight the theme of the uniqueness of Jesus Christ in the divine economy of salvation, something that would not have been necessary for other continents.

The changed self-perception of the Church and the new pastoral approach from below since Vatican II necessitates a new approach to mission. Rapid developments in human society and their impact on the environment made inevitable the question of how to do mission, or *how the Church can be mission*, in the twenty-first century.

Theologians and biblical exegetes may debate whether or not Jesus directly established the Church, but there can be no doubt whatsoever that Christ willed it. The faith of the Church from the very outset has been that the Church, concretized by his apostles and the other early disciples, cannot be separated from Christ. The Church exists as an extension of Christ himself sent into the world. The Church has a mission or, better still, the Church is the visible presence and continuation of Christ's mission in the world. The Church is Christ's message and is tasked by Christ to foster this message in every age until the end of time. What this means is that because the Church has been entrusted by Christ with his message to the world, it must itself be engulfed by the message in order to deliver it effectively. In a sense, the Church itself must become both the message and the messenger of Christ.

If this gift of Christ's message to and in the Church is for humanity in the world, it must be expressed historically. Thus, whatever happens in history affects the Church and Christian mission in one way or another. Questions concerning the content of the Church's faith in Christ, its context, and the methods of its proclamation remain permanently necessary, valid and relevant for the Church's survival and identity. This problematic question is intrinsic to the Church's mission. It finds radical expression first and foremost in Jesus himself. Jesus as God, the origin of the message entrusted to the Church, did not escape the implications of the questions concerning the expression of his message in time and space, relative to the content, context, and method of his message. Instead, he responded to them directly and thoroughly through the mystery of the Incarnation. God became human and situated Himself in human time and space, with everything which that condition implied "but sin." Likewise, the early disciples of Jesus faced similar questions. As happened when the faith and the Church began to spread outside their cradle of Palestine to other parts of the then Roman Empire, the Catholic faithful throughout the ages have had to confront questions and issues of content, context, and methods of evangelization.

Today, change is rapid and profound, described by such notions as "globalization," "secularization," or "secularism." As Pope John Paul II described it in his Encyclical Letter, *Redemptoris Missio* (no. 32), "today we face a . . . situation which is extremely varied and changing. Peoples are on the move; social and religious realities which were once clear and well defined are today increasingly complex." As illustrations, he writes: "We need only think of certain phenomena such as urbanization, mass migration, the flood of refugees, the de-Christianization of countries with ancient Christian traditions, the increasing influence of the Gospel and its values in overwhelmingly non-Christian countries, and the proliferation of messianic cults and religious sects." The Pope acknowledges that as a consequence, "religious and social upheaval makes it difficult to apply in practice certain ecclesial distinctions and categories to which we have become accustomed," especially in the field of mission.

This is the same point Pope Paul VI was making in *Evangelii Nuntiandi* (no. 3) when he observed that the conditions of every age necessitate the task of constant "re-envisioning" of Christ's message. Every period, according to Pope Paul VI also, obliges the Church "to revise methods, to seek by every means to study how we can bring the Christian message" into the heart of each human era. The Pope insists, nevertheless, that we must not do so at the expense of the truth of the Gospel of Christ, but by taking "into account a heritage of faith that the Church has the duty of preserving in its untouchable purity, and of presenting it to the people of our time, in a way that is as understandable and persuasive as possible."

Well into the third millennium of Christian existence, these circumstances confront the Church in new ways and impinge powerfully upon it. They force Christ's faithful to reconsider not only the understanding and articulation and formulation of the inviolable belief in Jesus as "Christ the Lord." Changed and changing spiritual and physical conditions in the historical realities where the message of Jesus must find a home call for this constant reconsideration. Furthermore, they demand a re-examination of the ways of bringing Jesus' message to people in the light of current knowledge about the world, about Jesus himself, and about his message. The process is intrinsic to the task of proclaiming the Gospel or evangelization. This task will be seriously affected in a negative way, Pope Paul VI argues in *Evangelii Nuntiandi* (no. 29), if it does "not take account of the unceasing interplay of the Gospel and of man's concrete life, both personal and social." For Pope Paul VI, "this is why evangelization involves an explicit message, adapted to the different situations constantly being realized . . . ." Therefore, the Pope insists that true evangelization must be comprehensive. It must also be concerned "about the rights and duties of every human being, about family life without which personal growth and development is hardly possible, about life in society, about international life, peace, justice and development . . . [and] about liberation."

Pope John Paul II in *Redemptoris Missio* (no. 52) is even more explicit about the relationship between culture and evangelization, insisting that evangelization must take culture seriously. "As she carries out missionary activity among the nations," he writes, "the Church encounters different cultures and becomes involved in the process of inculturation. The need for such involvement has marked the Church's pilgrimage throughout her history, but today it is particularly urgent." This is no easy task, and if we take inculturation in its broadest sense, it constitutes the appropriate method of all evangelization everywhere. As Pope John Paul II explains:

> The process of the Church's insertion into peoples' cultures is a lengthy one. It is not a matter of purely external adaptation, for inculturation "means the intimate transformation of authentic cultural values through their integration in Christianity and the insertion of Christianity in the various human cultures." The process is thus a profound and all-embracing one, which involves the Christian message and also the Church's reflection and practice. But at the same time it is a difficult process, for it must in no way compromise the distinctiveness and integrity of the Christian faith.

Through inculturation, the Church makes the Gospel incarnate in different cultures and at the same time introduces peoples, together with their cultures, into her own community. She transmits to them her own values, at the same time taking the good elements that already exist in them and renewing them from within. Through inculturation the Church, for her part, becomes a more intelligible sign of what she is, and a more effective instrument of mission.

Consequently, it is of the essence of mission that the messengers of the Gospel "immerse themselves in the cultural milieu of those to whom they are sent, moving beyond their own cultural limitations. Hence, they must learn the language of the place in which they work, become familiar with the most important expressions of the local culture, and discover its values through direct experience." It is only in this way that they will "be able to bring to people the knowledge of the hidden mystery . . . in a credible and fruitful way" (*Redemptoris Missio*, no. 53). Without this kind of missionary immersion into culture, past mistakes will be repeated. Lack of knowledge and respect for the presence of God in the other, makes "evangelization" to be trapped by too much condemnation, to the point of rejecting the inspiration of the Holy

Spirit in different cultures as foreign to divine action. The consequence of this is that the roots of evangelization will remain shallow.

The purpose of mission is to reveal Christ through the Church. In the words of Pope John Paul II, mission "is nothing other and nothing less than the manifestation or epiphany of God's plan and its fulfillment in the world and in history; in this history God, by means of missions, clearly accomplishes the history of salvation" (*Redemptoris Missio*, no. 41). Concretely, this consists in bringing about the prophetic vision which Jesus Christ described as the core of his mission—the realization of charity, justice, and peace, which are manifestations of the reign of God. This evangelizing mission of the Church must endure in history if the Church herself is to endure because mission forms the heart of the Church's life and the only reason for her existence.

According to St. Paul, the mission of proclaiming the Good News of Jesus is for the Church, not a choice; it is a responsibility imposed upon her by Christ himself. With this obligation in mind, Paul sees all other legitimate personal freedoms one may claim as subordinate to, or even as supplanted by, the duty of proclaiming Jesus. To the Philippians, he puts it dramatically, saying that in comparison to being in the service of Christ's message, everything else is "rubbish" (Phil 3:8), even life itself. This is the logic that leads him to cry out, "woe to me if I do not preach the Gospel" (1 Cor 9:16). Thus, Vatican II's assertion that "the pilgrim Church is missionary by her very nature" is unquestionable (*Ad Gentes*, no.2).

The appropriate theological perception of evangelization today is mission as "*missio Dei*"; the method is the imperative of dialogue; and human solidarity as the sign of the reign of God on earth and the goal of evangelization.

Mission is first of all God's activity. The Church participates in this prior divine action. "For, it is from the mission of the Son and the mission of the Holy Spirit," according to the Council, that the Church "takes her origin, in accordance with the decree of God the Father" (*Ad Gentes*). This is the mission the Church partakes in when it sends out messengers in the name of Christ "to preach not their own selves or their personal ideas, but a Gospel of which neither she nor they are the absolute masters and owners, to dispose of it as they wish, but a Gospel of which they are the ministers, in order to pass it on with complete fidelity" (*Evangelii Nuntiandi*, no. 15). This awareness frees the Church from treating Christ's message according to her own will and whim, as well as from the anxiety of trying to secure success of the message by her own power. Paul's disclaimer to the Church in Corinth of not "impressing" them by his own wisdom (1 Cor 2:1–5) is pertinent for every evangelizing situation.

The realization of mission as God's desire and initiative is for the Church an inspiration and incentive, "the source of our boldness, strength and joy as we participate in the *Missio Dei*," as A. Nasimiyu-Wasike and D. W. Waruta explain: "It is also the basis for our hope—hope not in human work but in God's work unfolding through human involvement."[6] Vatican II introduces the Decree on the Missionary Activity of the Church (*Ad Gentes*, no. 1) by affirming this position, that the proclamation of the Gospel throughout the universe is as much a requirement from Christ as it is part of the inner logic of the Church's "own catholicity." "For the Church was founded upon the apostles," the Council says, "who, following in the footsteps of Christ, 'preached the message of truth and begot churches.' Upon their successors devolves the duty of perpetuating this work through the years." This is for the sake of concretizing in the world the message of Christ or, in other words, establishing divine sovereignty on earth "as it is in heaven."

The implication for evangelization concerns the evangelizers' attitudes which in the past tended to place the evangelizer into the limelight. The point being underlined in the contemporary perception of mission is that there is no justification whatsoever for the Church as messenger to take credit for proclaiming the message. The servant should not expect special treatment for fulfilling his or her responsibilities. What is required of the Church is always to keep faith in the program the master has laid out and to maintain a keen sense of duty. In the end, the Church can only say, "I have done what I was supposed to do" (see Luke 17:7–10). This is why Paul again explicitly warns the Church at Corinth not to take personal credit for the work anyone has performed for Christ's Gospel. It is God that must take the credit in all cases, for spreading the message is primarily God's work. Like a mirror, the evangelizer must reflect the sun, and the sun here is the God of Jesus. Pope Paul VI in *Evangelii Nuntiandi* (no. 26) puts it this way:

> To evangelize is first of all to bear witness, in a simple and direct way, to God revealed by Jesus Christ, in the Holy Spirit, to bear witness that in His Son God has loved the world—that in His Incarnate Word He has given being to all things and has called . . . [persons] to eternal life. Perhaps this attestation of God will be for many people the unknown God whom they adore without giving Him a name, or whom they seek by a secret call of the heart. . . . But it is fully evangelizing in manifesting the fact that for . . . [human beings] the Creator is not an anonymous and remote power; He is the Father: ". . . that we should be called children of God; and so we are." And thus we are one another's brothers and sisters in God.

---

6. Nasimiyu-Wasike and Waruta, "Introduction," 1.

This requirement of being totally at the service of God, concretized as disinterested love and communion through dialogue, applies directly to the identity and mission of the Church in our time. All of Christ's faithful are called to this witness, even in silence (*Evangelii Nuntiandi*, no. 21). Through their life, the follower of Christ can inspire questions in others which lead to Christ. This is the dialogue of life which, given the right conditions, may lead to the dialogue of words or doctrine.

Anglican Bishop Michael Nazir-Ali affirms that today, "the whole Christian mission, however it is exercised, is founded on this kind of dialogue; it is the basis for community and incorporates "law and order and justice"; "the distribution of resources"; "fair trade"; "the need for peace." The whole of life is the scope of the Church's dialogue of action in mission. The Church must dialogue with the political order; with the scientific community; with the arts; with other faiths and religions and ideologies. If there is "a common spiritual quest in which we are all engaged," the Church must ask, "what is the unique Christian contribution to this?"[7]

The Church emphasized the propositional, verbal, or doctrinal mode of evangelization in the past to the point of imposing ideas, symbols, and language where the other was hardly offered a chance to respond. Although preaching the message demands doctrinal formulation, it is not necessarily the only or even first step in the process. The "dialogue of life, in which people communicate by way of their actions, inspiring others to imitate or reject certain modes of looking at and living life, or even just to reflect on its merits and demerits" is equally important.[8] This leads to respect of the other, even in spite of acknowledged differences and the possibility of rejecting the new worldview. But respect is fundamental for genuine evangelization. The required mixture of propositional dialogue and the dialogue of life is again demonstrated by Paul in his speech at the Areopagus in Athens. While deeply and genuinely full of admiration for the Athenians' religiosity, Paul draws them to the vision of the message of Christ (Acts 17:22–31). For the missionary, it is important to bear in mind the conclusion that Luke gives as a result of the speech: "When they heard about the resurrection of the dead, some began to scoff, but others said, 'We should like to hear you on this some other time . . . .' But some did join him and became believers" (Acts 17:32–34).

The series of questions that Pope Paul VI poses to anyone preaching the message of Christ are vital to the process of evangelization as dialogue: "Do you really believe what you are proclaiming? Do you live what you believe? Do you really preach what you live? The witness of life has become more than ever

---

7. Nazir-Ali, *Mission and Dialogue*, 58–59.
8. Magesa, *African Religion in the Dialogue*, 59–60.

an essential condition for real effectiveness in preaching. Precisely because of this we are, to a certain extent, responsible for the progress of the Gospel that we proclaim" (*Evangelii Nuntiandi*, no. 76). For, according to the Pope, "Modern man listens more willingly to witnesses than to teachers, and if he does listen to teachers, it is because they are witnesses" (no. 41).

Solidarity and communion are signs of the Church's authentic mission. For a long time, the Church tended to define her distinctiveness and the specificity of her mission in terms of opposition, of "we" against "them." Often justifying this contrast on the basis of faith in the uniqueness of Christ and his message, the process almost always ended up breeding sectarian attitudes, or becoming ideological. Ideology involves the narrow-minded rationalization of one's own position, and coercively and arbitrarily imposing it over others as the norm. In these instances, the Church herself acted and was perceived as an ideologue. The history of evangelization in Africa has traces of this mistake. The authentic message of Christ is antithetical to violence and coercion of any form and for whatever goal. Its goal is inclusion. "What amazes one again and again," as Bosch points out, "is the inclusiveness of Jesus' mission. . . . His mission is one of dissolving alienation and breaking down walls of hostility, of crossing boundaries between individuals and groups."[9] This inclusiveness, without discrimination on any grounds whatsoever, was what became "revolutionary" when it was adopted by the Christian movement at the behest of the Holy Spirit. It gave the new movement its mark of identity which was admired by some and vilified by others.

Exclusion is bred by the attitude of "fundamentalism." Leonardo Boff explains the fundamentalist as "one who sees himself or herself as the holder of an absolute truth, and thus is destined to intolerance." But "intolerance causes contempt for the other, and contempt engenders aggression, and aggression brings wars to combat and exterminate those who have erred."[10] As such, fundamentalism of any kind is inimical to true Christian evangelization and the building of God's reign on earth.

The Church as a Eucharistic community is something that has to be expressed in love in the lives of the faithful, beginning with the domestic Church. The great variety of peoples and situations in the contemporary world, brought close together as never before by modern technology, makes this task extremely challenging. It is reminiscent of the 1st century presence to one another of "Jew and Roman, Greek and barbarian, free and slave, rich and poor, woman and man."[11] We may speak today, for example, of

---

9. Bosch, *Transforming Mission*, 28.
10. Boff, *Fundamentalism, Terrorism*, 15.
11. Bosch, *Transforming Mission*, 48.

Christians and Muslims, Catholics and Protestants, Africans and Europeans, straight and gay people, HIV-infected persons and others, as the modern equivalents of Jews, Greeks, and so on in the early Church. The point is the need to form community of all of these disparate groups as the vital element of Jesus' mission and consequently the mission of the Church or the Church as mission. The Church cannot continue to identify itself by exclusion, but as a servant or witness of the love of God for humanity and the universe as a whole, through Jesus the Christ.

Chapter 10

The Public Role of the Church in Contemporary Africa

THE STRUGGLE FOR SUBJECTIVITY and identity forms part of the growth of every person or any corporate body. As a corporate body, the Church has had to face this challenge from the very beginning of its existence, initially vis-à-vis Judaism and the gentile religions, and then against Roman imperial-religious power as well as the dominant philosophies of the day. The early development of doctrine was a result of this struggle. But the process cannot end because the Church as a living organism in a changing environment continues to evolve. The question for Africa is, what is involved in being Church in Africa today, especially in the socio-political arena? In our age of sharply conflicting interests, the Church has to be clear about its position in the areas of political, economic, and social structures and ideologies. To the extent that it fails this or is ambiguous about it, to that extent is its mission compromised. "Identity refers to commitment and loyalty of a particular culture, religion, or community," as Aquiline Tarimo explains.

> It is a medium through which people define themselves vis-à-vis other groups as well as reinforce patterns of social relationships between members of a given community. Identity defines social space; it forms part of the normal process of growth and development of a specific identity. No individual or corporate body is completely identical to another; differences identify who or what one is. They provide "personality." They constitute identity markers. Individuals and corporate bodies remain different from one another, regardless

of membership to a family, ethnic group, nation, club, creed, or any other biological or sociological association.[1]

In voluntary associations, conscious choice is usually the main factor of identity; it is the fundamental aspect of belonging and loyalty. The question usually is this, to what kind of group does one want to belong and in pursuit of what end? This is a question of vision, process and goal. It refers to a group's character. Character, in the broad sense of the concept, is the all-embracing identity-marker that subsumes all others. We can speak of the "character" of either individuals or corporate bodies to define them, to point them out for what they really are, and to distinguish them from other similar entities.

Just like other groups, the Church cannot be the same in every place at all times. Though possessing the same general characteristic as the Church of Christ, as localized bodies local Churches sport certain particular identity-markers. It is possible to speak of the *identities* of Christian Churches in various locations and times. For instance, in the New Testament, the existence of different Churches, with different characteristics in terms of theologies is quite clear and seems to be taken for granted. Most of the apostles preach to the Jews, but Peter and Paul and Barnabas to the Gentiles. This seems to have been the acknowledged consensus in the Apostolic Church. Further, it is customary to speak with reference to the New Testament of the Johannine or Pauline Churches, and in the case of the latter, Christian assemblies quite distinct from one another, each with particular organization, problems, and strengths.

Paul in his letters refers to the various Churches by name: the Church in Rome, Corinth, Ephesus, Philippi, and Galatia, as well as others which are home-based. In his letters too, Paul spells out the problems and virtues of each, the things that make him sad and those that make him happy. In fact, the letters are written to address some of the problems and strengths Paul recognizes to be brought about in the Churches he founded by different circumstances. New Testament scholarship has established that the different styles of writing and content that we find in the Gospels, the Acts of the Apostles, and the various Epistles indicate different social, political and economic environments, which form the context conditioning the development of the ecclesial identities of the early Churches that the apostles founded.

So, what is the identity of the Christian Church as an institution, a corporate body, or a community in Africa? The identity of the Church in Africa today is shaped by its reaction to what happens around it, indicating at the same time what happens within it. It is essential first to be clear about what

---

1. See Tarimo and Manwelo, *Ethnicity, Conflict*, 36.

THE PUBLIC ROLE OF THE CHURCH IN CONTEMPORARY AFRICA

context the Church in Africa finds itself in. How does it respond to this context? In the process of contact and the dynamics of mutual affirmation and rejection of elements between the Church and the surrounding milieu, Christian identity is formed.

If we are to look back to history at the end of the nineteenth century, what do we see? Two dominant aspects of the prevailing environment will be noted. On the one hand, there are strong traditional cultures in place. Although cultural contact with the outside world was not completely absent until then, it had barely affected traditional cultures, specifically in the religious arena. Africans prayed and worshipped in their indigenous ways, and questions were neither asked nor thought entertained about changing or modifying them. On the other hand, this was also the beginning of the establishment of the colonies, which formed the other side of the contextual coin where the Christian Church had to situate itself. It was a situation that was generally hostile toward the traditional social context at almost all levels: political, economic, and religious.

The political, commercial, and social interests of the new situation were at odds with their counterparts in the old. This conflict created an atmosphere of hostility, sometimes open, as in the Maji Maji and, later, Mau Mau struggles in Tanganyika and Kenya respectively. However, more often the discontent was simmering and much more permanent, and the identity of the protagonists was often defined in the struggle. For the Church, the question was how it could establish its unique identity in the context of these competing perceptions and ways of life? How should it navigate between the two worlds? On one side, there was the traditional context of political administration by leaders who also wielded sacred power, ancestor veneration, belief in spiritual presence everywhere, and customs not only different from, but strange to European perceptions. On the other, there was the European desire to "civilize the natives" through commerce and the introduction of new religious beliefs and behaviors.

History offers a picture of the Church's choice in this dilemma. By and large, it chose to side with the colonial context in its "civilizing mission of the natives." In other words, it blessed the colonial context with very little critique. Largely, it did not create a new context based on God's word in the Scriptures. Its identity was thus blurred among the majority of Africans who usually felt themselves unable to distinguish between the colonial political dispensation and the new Christian evangelical one, although the latter claimed to disassociate itself from the former. In different ways, this is the legacy the Church is still struggling with today.

When political independence came to Africa in the decade of the 1960s, the colonial-versus-traditional conflicting situation remained fundamentally unchanged in the cultural-social, political, and economic levels. This has contributed to shape the identity of the Church today. They also indicate ways in which it should define its identity in the future.

In the cultural-religious sphere, the identity of the Christian Churches is approached differently. The new charismatic Pentecostal and neo-Pentecostal branches of Christianity seem to define themselves in radical opposition to African religiosity and spirituality.[2] For these Churches, once one has been "born again," has "met Jesus," or been "saved," one must abandon almost *in toto* the African worldview. In this position, Pentecostal and neo-Pentecostal identity enjoys the voice and stance of clarity. The only question is at what cost? The price people have to pay for this stance is alienation from their roots. The benefits they seem to reap in terms of "healing," "deliverance," and "economic prosperity" are usually short-lived, probably because the identity thus formed does not send deep enough roots into cultural spirituality.

Opposition to the religious sensibilities of traditional value systems also still defines mainline Protestant and Catholic identity in Africa. If the missionary approach of blatant and total condemnation has been toned down, it is not in the areas that really matter. In the fields of ancestor veneration, the unity of the visible and spiritual universes, and similar issues of belief important to the general African Christian, the Christian Churches' position is still worlds apart from that of the African traditional reality. The African Christian still feels basically at a loss to identify oneself at the same time as African and Christian, something that the official position of the mainline Churches encourages. What they seem unable to do is to bring this about for fear of losing their identity through what is sometimes referred to as "relativism" and "syncretism."

But if the task of the Gospel of Christ is to challenge culture, it needs to construct a new culture, constantly. However, this new culture will happen only in the process of borrowing values from the cultural experiences around. For Africa, what this means is that Christ must be born anew in African cultures and live, preach, and die in this context. In this way, he brings out what is best in this culture. This is why "syncretism," understood not as liberal compromise but, positively, as the fusion of what is life-giving and life-enhancing from both Christian and African spiritual traditions, may be what is needed if there is to be an African Christianity, a new identity, one that is neither essentially European nor exclusively indigenous-African, but precisely *African-Christian*. As mentioned in a previous chapter of

2. See Shorter and Njiru. *New Religious Movements*, 2001.

this book, this is what most African Initiated Churches (AICs) struggle to achieve, with different degrees of success.

Some analyses and critiques of AICs have often focused on their failures, their emphasis on Old Testament biblical tradition at one extreme, or on African traditional spiritual practices at the other. These are indeed serious shortcomings and must be critiqued. But what is clear and admirable in the struggle the AICs are engaged in is the general vision they espouse. Contrary to some perceptions, theirs is not the "anything goes" type of exercise it is sometimes alleged to be. It is rather, in many cases, a struggle at conscientious and judicious reading, interoperation, adjudication, and fusion of the meaning of two texts: the text of the African life experience on the one hand, and the text of the Good News of Jesus Christ as found in the Scriptures on the other. This is the procedure that can provide us a new Christian identity in the African cultural context where, especially in this age of globalization, western and Black African philosophical and spiritual perceptions on life are more visibly in conflict than ever before.

The most obvious feature of the mainline Churches in the social sphere has been their clarity and distinctiveness of commitment to service, historically evidenced in the areas of education and health. Church-run schools have excelled in providing quality education throughout the African continent. The same can be said of the health sector as well, with the Churches establishing health facilities in many cases rivaling or exceeding those of the state in size and quality of service. With the eruption of the HIV/AIDS epidemic since 1983, the Churches have been quite clear about their rejection of the use of condoms as a way to tackle and arrest the pandemic. They have been severely criticized for this stance. Of course, whether or not the arguments they advance are correct can and perhaps should be debated. The point here is, however, that the position of the Churches, their identity on this issue, is unambiguous.

If the struggle for the identity of the Churches vis-à-vis African traditional spirituality may be considered an intra-Church affair, usually involving inner beliefs and teachings of religion, their political involvement touches directly the public sphere. It attracts much wider attention and, in Africa, it is often accompanied by vitriol from the state, especially when it is critical. The doctrine of "separation of church and state" preached in secular states around the world has much to recommend it, but is valid only up to a point. Conversely, the Church's claim that it has "nothing to do with politics," as well as some politicians' charge that it should not "meddle in politics," holds water only so far. Much of any Church's behavior cannot but be or at least appear "political." Since the state and the Church have society as their context, absolute categories of separation of involvement and activities cannot be sustained. Here also, the Church struggles for its own identity in muddled waters. Many factors are involved that constrain different Churches to identify themselves differently. Here are examples from one region of the continent.

In Kenya, the National Council of Churches of Kenya (NCCK) was at one time a fierce critic of then President Daniel arap Moi's regime for its alleged oppression and muzzling of dissent. The Africa Inland Church (AIC), however, left the NCCK over the issue because it perceived this body as biased against the president, an AIC member. Archbishop Ondiek of Legio Maria, an African Initiated Church, was at one time a minister in Moi's government, obviously putting the weight of the Church behind it. The Pentecostal World Intercessory Ministries and the NCCK were at loggerheads in 1992 over Moi's disputed re-election results, with the former urging that the results be accepted against the position of the latter. As Christian bodies, what and where was their identity?

In Kenya again, a similar scenario repeated itself with the controversial presidential elections, held in December 2007, which both Mwai Kibaki and Raila Odinga soon afterwards claimed to have won. The top leadership of the Catholic Church in Kenya was publicly divided along ethnic lines, thus putting exclusionary tribal identity ahead of inclusive Christian identity and commitment. According to Agbonkhianmeghe E. Orobator, the Church's "moral capacity" and "credibility" "to challenge society and uphold principles of right and wrong, truth and falsity" had been "severely eroded" in the situation. By colluding with unethical political leaders, the Church had compromised its "prophetic voice and provides cover for the state's unethical machinations."[3]

For Rwanda, the question involves the role the Churches played during the genocide of 1994 and the years leading to this tragic event. The trials at the International Criminal Tribunal for Rwanda in Arusha, Tanzania, indicated that, with a few notable exceptions, many of the Christian Churches in their top representatives were in one way or another accomplices to the situation leading to the crimes committed during the tragedy in that country. The orgy of brutal killings lasted for one hundred days and cost over 800,000 lives. In other words, the Church failed to distinguish itself as an entity with a different message from that which was brewing before 1994, one of tribal stereotyping and crude propaganda. If the political context in Rwanda for many years was one of hatred and vindictiveness and the use of political power for reasons of tribal discrimination and oppression, where was the voice of the Church? More precisely, what was the voice of the Church? Especially in a context such as Rwanda, silence was clearly a form of speech.

3. Orobator, "Church, State, and Catholic Ethics," 182–85.

What distinguishes the Church of Christ in every situation is intolerance against evil at whatever cost to itself.

The same general question applies to the situation in Tanzania and Uganda. During the long experimentation with *Ujamaa* socialism in Tanzania, what kind of voice did the Church offer? The relationship of the Catholic Church with a devout and practicing Catholic Christian president spearheading this experiment provides interesting study. With reference to *Ujamaa*, perhaps the only example of a firm and public stance in the Catholic Church's leadership was Bishop Christopher Mwoleka of Rulenge. The national association of bishops, the Tanzania Episcopal Conference (TEC), was obviously unsure about and prevaricated over the *Ujamaa* experiment throughout Nyerere's long tenure at the helm of the nation. It issued no clear statement one way or the other to explain its position at a time when the general population, mostly non-literate and confused about the direction the country was taking, needed guidance.

In Idi Amin's reign of terror in Uganda, a celebrated example of the Church's position was Archbishop Janani Luwum of the Church of Uganda who, unsurprisingly, paid for it with his life. Unlike in Tanzania, the position for which Archbishop Luwum died was initially collective. In September 1976, at a meeting of all the bishops of the Church of Uganda, the Catholic Church, and prominent leaders of the Muslim community, Archbishop Luwum was elected chairman. The meeting surveyed major aspects of national life under the Amin regime and denounced the performance of the government in very clear terms. This meeting would spell the fate of the Archbishop. "Amin, when he obtained the minutes of this meeting, was furious, and also nervous lest the religious leaders should unite against him." He etched the plan to have the Archbishop eliminated. After the murder of Archbishop Luwum, the Church of Uganda made a complete about-turn and placed at the head of the Church bishops "who have not had the courage of Luwum! And this has been done deliberately, apparently to safeguard the Church's position in the good books of each succeeding regime."[4] It is not difficult to see how the identity of the Church of Uganda as an independent entity was thereby seriously compromised.

How about the identity of the Church in the economic realm? Economically, Africa is poor. Most of the highly indebted poor countries of the world are to be found here. When the media and human rights organizations talk of people who live under a dollar a day, it is in most instances Africa they are referring to. And Africa is on the agenda whenever the rich industrialized nations meet to discuss issues of international aid.

---

4. Gifford, *African Christianity*, 119–21.

It is true that the Church cannot do much directly in this field. But "directly" is an important qualifier, because the poverty of Africa is caused by factors that the Church can indirectly influence. These factors are mostly ethical and involve also Christians. Reference here is to the corruption of people in high places. Embezzling public funds or funds provided for development projects by donors is one form of rampant corruption bedeviling Africa. The necessary money does not reach its targets in building the necessary infrastructures that could speed up the industrialization and the development of the African nations. Instead, it simply disappears into the pockets of the already wealthy, so that the gap between the few rich and the majority poor widens by the day. Cases of corruption constitute the daily headlines of the media in almost all African countries. This is not a new phenomenon; it comes to the forefront of the public only because of the freedom of the press in contrast to the totalitarianism that was in place previously. There is a "culture of impunity" where none of the crimes of corruption are prosecuted and punished.

This is not an exaggeration. To hear that Members of Parliament in a poor African country are some of the highest paid representatives in the world baffles the imagination, and this at a time when many of the people they represent die daily of malnutrition. Reportedly, the type, size, and number of vehicles for many Eastern African leaders bought at public expense rival those of their counterparts from the donor countries Africa constantly asks for economic aid. Occasionally here, a president has aroused national fury because he wants to buy a state-of-the-art personal jet at huge public expense.

However, all of this fades into the background compared to the corrupt deals African governments make, virtually selling their countries to outside, wealthy interests, and thus putting the existence of Africa's future generations in jeopardy. The sale of huge tracts of land to foreign transnational corporations is one such instance, and is reportedly not limited to one or two countries in the continent. There are also the mining and drilling concessions where the same thing happens. One of the most well-known cases is the drilling of oil in the Niger Delta of Nigeria. But perhaps the most heinous of all concerns those deals that allow the transfer and dumping of poisonous waste materials from foreign industries onto African soil. The immediate consequences in terms of people killed or maimed are bad enough, but the long-term ones in terms of harm to human health and the environment brought to future generations are indescribably unconscionable.

In the economic sphere as well, the role of the Church should be clear. For the Church's identity is expressed most clearly in defense of life and the protection of God's universe. How, then, does the Church treat those of its members who are known embezzlers, or who conclude murderous deals such as the above? Public censure would certainly not contravene the spirit of the Gospel. The goal would not be to keep the people in question outside the fold of the Church: we are all sinners and need the mercy and grace of God. But the Church also has to show the need for repentance.

There are happy historical precedents of religious groups taking serious action against blatant injustice, exploitation, and oppression by their members. The example of the Quakers (or Society of Friends) and the North American Episcopal Methodist Church's rejection of the institution of slavery as intrinsically evil comes to mind. As John F. Maxwell reports, towards the end of the eighteenth century, the Methodists had rejected slavery. They described it as "contrary to the laws of God, man, and nature, and hurtful to society; contrary to the dictates of conscience and pure religion and doing that which we would not others should do to us or ours." Maxwell observes: "In 1785 all slave-holding members of this Church were given 12 months in which to emancipate their slaves or quietly withdraw from the Church. Those who disposed of them in any other way than emancipation were to be expelled from the Episcopal Methodist Church. This rule was reaffirmed in 1801."[5]

Modern-day slaveholders—the corrupt government officials—might not think much of this kind of action from the Church against them. They may just ignore it and consider themselves none the worse for it. But it would be an important symbol of integrity of the Church as a whole to the world. When the Church embraces them or, in one way or another, it benefits from them, its mission is compromised. To be able to play a meaningful role in resolving some of the serious problems brought about by conflicting interests in Africa, the Church needs to have a clear image. A fragmented image with fragmented loyalties will only play into the hands of those who advance fragmented ethnic or tribal loyalties, and this for ends that may actually be inimical to African nationhood, rights and dignity.

The image of the Church should be built on the principle that Christians are people who identify themselves primarily by their concern for justice and truth. And it will be defined by where it puts its institutional weight in conflicting interests. It is often said that the Church should not take sides in social and political issues, that it should be "neutral." This may be true, but only to a point. Certainly, the Church should not be a "political party," or engage in partisan politics, or espouse partisan ideologies. But that is as far as it goes. To take this axiom further is not only to obfuscate the identity of the Church; it is to compromise and frustrate her mission. In reality, to be neutral in matters of consequence is not to be neutral at all; and not to take sides is to take one. Someone will always claim the Church's weight in these situations, when it

---

5. Maxwell, *Slavery and the Catholic Church*, 96.

would be much better off for the Church to utter its own voice based on its own autonomy, informed choice, prophecy, and advocacy.

The very essence of individuation and identity is autonomy. Without autonomy there is no real identity. Autonomy means the capacity to choose, that is, to make decisions. It is possible to suppress autonomy, either forcibly or by way of indoctrination or bribery, so that the decision-making faculty in an individual or community is compromised. Autocratic and dictatorial rulers hate autonomy and do everything in their power to eliminate it. But if the Church is to guarantee its true identity as guardian of justice, human rights and dignity, it must jealously protect its autonomy to speak and act. The source of its autonomy is to be found in God's Word. Divine revelation and inspiration are always difficult to interpret, and sometimes the Church experiences failure in this task. Yet the only sure criterion of correct interpretation of God's will for humankind and the universe consists in the principle of promotion of life in love. "God is love." If the Church must err, let her err on the side of love and service to life. Concern for life here on earth is the Church's mandate. The Church is nothing if not the sacrament or visible sign of life.

The problem for the autonomy of the Church in Africa is twofold: African leaders often solicit the favor of the Church on the one hand, and Church leaders sometimes solicit favors from the state on the other. This has often compromised the autonomy of the Church to speak. True autonomy demands that the Church must denounce evil or affirm love-justice without fear or favor. Paul instructs Timothy as leader in the Church that his true calling is to "proclaim the word; [to] be persistent whether it is convenient or inconvenient; [to] convince, reprimand, encourage through all patience and teaching." There will be obstacles, of course, "but you, be self-possessed in all circumstances; put up with hardship; perform the work of an evangelist; fulfill your ministry" (see 2 Tim 4:2, 5). This is the kind of ministry Jesus ascribed to himself, the ministry of freeing everyone who is in the bondage of evil. It is the ministry at the service of truth that sets people free.

Autonomy is the foundation of prophecy, understood here as speaking on behalf of God. Autonomy, in Christian terms, means placing oneself before God alone and being ready to be used by God: "Here I am, Lord, send me." The biblical prophetic literature is clear on one point: speaking in the name of God often has painful consequences. Yet, when things are not right in society, especially when the poor and helpless suffer, God calls forth prophets to point out wrongdoing and explain what God wants. The Church should be such a prophetic voice today. If there is any ministry the Church desperately needs now in Africa, it is the ministry of prophecy. As President Jomo Kenyatta advised the Catholic Bishops of Eastern Africa their plenary meeting in Nairobi in 1976, "The Church is the conscience of society, and today a society needs a conscience. Do not be afraid to speak. If we are wrong and you keep quiet, one day you may have to answer for our mistakes."[6] Continuing he said:

> One of the services you give to others is to help keep them going in the right direction. We may have many distractions and can wander off the path. We do need to be constantly put back on it again. Then, too, most of us are not theologians, and in the complexities of modern life, we may not even know we are going astray, that we are making the wrong decision. That is why we need the Church in our midst to tell us when we are making a mistake.[7]

In the continent, there have been such voices, but in most cases they have not been sustained. The Old Testament prophetic figure shouts until people listen. Regardless of personal imperfections, Bishop Pius Ncube of Zimbabwe must be listed as an example of Christian prophecy when he pointed out the ills of the regime.[8] Leaders who denounce oppression and discrimination in Africa must expect their imperfections to be exposed by the enemies of truth. What is crucial for the Church's identity is that it must support the prophets among its children. No one is perfect. But does that excuse anyone from denouncing evil? God works with saints and sinners alike; the choice is God's. We cannot expect that the Church must be completely perfect before it engages in the prophetic task of denouncing injustice.

Nevertheless, it is necessary to mention that the Church's credibility will be enhanced if it denounces also injustice within its own system. The importance of this requirement cannot be overemphasized. The 1971 Synod said as much in its concluding document, "Justice in the World." The statement was radical: the Church should not presume to talk to others about justice unless it is just in people's eyes. The Church must bear this in mind if its stewardship of the Gospel is not to be despised as hypocritical. Introspection in the sense of sincere self-examination is part and parcel of Christian prophecy.

To be able to announce God's word for the salvation of the world, the Church needs to inform herself as deeply as possible on the issues at hand and pray for the assistance of the Holy Spirit to guide it. Can the Church pronounce on economics? Can it say anything about politics? Does it have the experts or expertise to do so? The Church may not, and perhaps should not, portray itself as having specific solutions to specific political or economic problems. Even Popes have pointed this out a number of times.

---

6. Mejia, *Conscience of Society*, 50.
7. Mejia, *Conscience of Society*, 6.
8. Bishop Ncube was spied on and exposed by the regime for sexual immorality.

Nevertheless, the Church's faith gives it a certain confidence to point out evil. What special expertise is needed to see oppression, marginalization, and suffering among people?

Prophecy for the Church today, in the sense of pronouncing the word of God in affirmation or denunciation of given situations caused by human agency, means putting the Church's institutional weight behind its declarations. In other words, it involves the ministry of advocacy. It should not relegate this responsibility completely to secular non-governmental organizations (NGOs). This is not to say that NGOs have no place in advocacy; it is rather to say that the Church does it from the specific perspective of its faith in the liberating power of Jesus Christ. It approaches the issue from a different angle, one that is part of its identity. This can make all the difference.

Aquiline Tarimo quotes Donal Dorr to the effect that the Catholic Church may be standing "under the judgment of... [its] own social teaching" which it has developed "fairly comprehensively" over many years. The question is how it puts this teaching into practice; how it lives it. How concretely does it side with the oppressed in Africa? Tarimo suggests that one way to do this is to uplift the awareness of the masses. For this, the Church needs more effective methods of bringing its message where it is needed to create "public impact." Could the Church cooperate with NGOs in this task? According to Tarimo, "without this cooperation the entire effort of transforming social structures will not bring forth the desired fruits."[9]

In 1979, Adrian Hastings observed something that still holds true in many parts of Africa: after years of independence, "politics have become a bad joke" in the eyes of many due to corruption and pure bad governance, so that people do not really identify with the political administrations in place. The Churches, however, seem in comparison to have "grown in popular credibility as much as the governments have declined in that commodity." In personalities like Archbishop Janani Luwum, the Churches seem to attract the confidence of the masses and so exert considerable influence with the people. Hastings notes that "many a government continues to find that there is no reasonable alternative to accepting this fact of life and keeping what ecclesiastical friends it may." The question is how the Church will use this influence, its "institutional weight."[10]

Julius K. Nyerere answered this question in very clear, unambiguous language. He asserted that the task of the Church is to participate "actively" in the process of "rebellion against those social structures and economic organizations which condemn... [human beings] to poverty, humiliation and degradation."

9. Tarimo, *Applied Ethics and Africa's Social Reconstruction*, 103.
10. Hastings, *History of African Christianity*, 263.

Failing this, according to Nyerere, the Church becomes "irrelevant," "and the Christian religion will degenerate into a set of superstitions accepted by the fearful. Unless the Church, its members and organizations, express God's love for . . . [human beings] by involvement and leadership in constructive protest against the present conditions . . . then it will become identified with injustice and persecution."[11] In its mission to advance God's reign here on earth, the Church should not construct its identity based on "safe," "polite," or "popular" decisions, but on conscientiously "right" ones.

---

11. Nyerere, *Freedom and Development*, 215–16.

Chapter 11

The Public Face of Theology

UNDERLYING THE PUBLIC ROLE of the Church in society is the role of theology. The Social Teaching of the Church (STC) plays a pivotal role in guiding the Church in this matter, but so should theology in general.

Theology as reflection on the relationship between God and humanity assumes two dimensions; the absence of any one of which impoverishes it. Theology makes demands on the life of the individual believer to enter into a closer relationship with Transcendence. This implies an on-going endeavor toward personal inner spiritual transformation. Christian theology refers to this as the process of "conversion"—a life-long task. The effort constitutes the vertical dimension of theology, how one should conduct one's relationship with God, something that is achieved through prayer and other forms of ritual. But theology necessarily bears also a social dimension, concerning shared conversion. This level of change connotes the transformation, not only of the individual heart, but also established social structures that play a crucial role in the transformation of the heart. In other words, the individual, personal facet of intimacy with God can hardly be achieved if and when social communion is lacking, if and when structures systemically obstruct this goal. Theology strives to articulate and clarify the significance, for the Christian, of both dimensions of the faith: the personal and the social. The reign of God that theology promotes is ultimately a social goal. The Book of Revelation (7:1ff. and 14:1ff.), for instance, symbolically portrays the unity of the personal and social levels of God's reign as a great assembly of people before God.

Thus, authentic Christian theology cannot relinquish its horizontal social responsibility. For this reason, it is proper to speak of the public role of theology, by which is meant the implications of the contemplation of God on the actual social, political, and economic life of a particular community and, indeed, increasingly today, the entire human race and the universe. How should these be organized in a manner that promotes God's reign of justice, peace and reconciliation in the here and now? Of the many scriptural sources that impel this theological task, perhaps the most revealing is God's own words to Moses as he sent him on the mission to rescue Israel from mistreatment and indignity: "I have . . . seen the misery of my people in Egypt. I have heard them crying out because of their slave drivers, and I am concerned about their suffering. So I have come down to rescue them" (Exod 3:7–8). This divine concern applies to all people suffering injustice.

The question of theology in the public sphere, therefore, pertains to the role of faith and religion in politics. Figuratively speaking, where is the connection between the "Altar," representing faith in Christ essentially as life in the world according to the mind or will of God, and the "Palace," symbolizing structures and institutions for governance arising from human beliefs and philosophies?

From the beginning, the Church and religion and the political establishment have not made very good bedfellows; they cannot always be completely reconciled. When the Pharisees inquired of Jesus whether it was legitimate to pay taxes to the civil authorities, Jesus retorted: "give back to Caesar what is Caesar's, and to God what is God's" (Matt 22:21, Mark 12:17, Luke 20:25). In terms of the interaction between the Altar and the Palace, Jesus' response must be understood to mean: Obey civil authorities only when they do not interfere with the authority of God. Thus understood, the remark touches on the relationship between civil society and Christian communities of faith which theology is there to serve. It means that faith in Christ and theology must offer some direction to human social living in the world.

It is not possible to overlook the tension reflected in the words of Jesus between the two domains of human existence: temporal power ("Caesar") and the order of faith in the ultimate supreme authority of God (invested in ecclesiastical leadership or the "Altar"). It is true that Paul directs the Christian faithful in Rome to obey civil leaders because, as he puts it, "all authority comes from God, and those in positions of authority have been placed there by God" (Rom 13:1). He argues that "anyone who rebels against authority is rebelling against what God has instituted, and they will be punished" (Rom 13:2). About this order, exegetes point out that Paul is addressing a specific context. "Up to the time that Paul writes . . . there has been no official persecution of Christianity in Rome"; there has not been much visible conflict between the young Christian community and the Roman civil authorities of the day. Moreover, "the supposition" constituting the directive "is that the civil authorities are conducting themselves rightly and are seeking the interests of the community."[1]

Paul in this passage does not discuss particulars of governance, such as the question of obedience to "a tyrannical government or one failing to cope with a situation where the just rights of individual citizens or of a minority group are neglected or violated." Rather, it is the general principle of the "duty of subjects to legitimate authority" that occupies him at the moment. As he sees it, the power of civil authorities to work for the common good is delegated to them from God, thus the obligation of Christians to obey them. Again, a different scenario where human dignity and rights are infringed or neglected is not envisaged here by Paul.[2]

Even in Paul's counsel, one can already see the tension between the Palace and the Altar, between the secular mind in the business of governance and the framework of life in the world inspired by Christian faith. Civil power may be unmindful of the fact that its authority is delegated to it from God for the purpose of authentic human flourishing as the desired order of human social existence in the universe. Thus, given the presence of the two social realities, the Church and the state, how should they interact? Concretely: Is there a place for Christian imagination in secular governance? Even more directly: What is the role of Christian theology in the organization and running of the state?

More than ever before, this is a complex question today because no state is homogenous. Most national entities are constituted of a multiplicity of identities that are multi-ethnic, multi-cultural, multiclass, and multi-religious. How might Christian theology play a role in inspiring a just society while recognizing the autonomy of the state in organizing these identities? Can Christian theology claim to have a "right" to work to transform society after the blueprint painted by the Gospels? This claim is legitimate and necessary. It has its foundation in the Scriptures. The Christian faith has everything to do with practical life: faith must seek life. This is what Christian theology must always spell out. It must articulate for the world what it means to "act justly, to love mercy and walk humbly with God" (Mic 6:8).

The rationality of abundance of life that Jesus insists he came to bring into the world (John 10:10) amounts to the assertion that the copiousness of life is what must be demonstrated by theology as a universal goal. It constitutes the task of theology in the first place as "faith seeking understanding" (*fides quaerens intellectum*), as Anselm of Canterbury, phrased it. But life in

---

1. See Fitzmyer, "The Letter to the Romans," 864.
2. Fitzmyer, "The Letter to the Romans," 1.

abundance can be concretely approximated only through actual programs dedicated to a community of love and generated through socio-political structures of good governance. For this reason, theology must challenge mentalities and attitudes that construct structures that do not measure up to this standard even while acknowledging that all human structures fall short of God's standards. Structures must continuously be reformed to bring them as close as possible to the divine ideal.

Apart from Jesus himself, the Epistles of James and John both argue very forcefully that God cannot be honored if the tangible human being is not. In the specific and rather strong expression of the First Epistle of John, "Whoever claims to love God yet hates a brother or sister is a liar. For whoever does not love their brother and sister, whom they have seen, cannot love God, whom they have not seen" (1 John 4:20). James for his part paints a clear and pragmatic picture of the demand for social action (Jas 2:16-20).

The point for theology is the explication of what the Christian vocation must be in the world. The manner through which the mercy of God is pragmatically experienced in the world is far from being a superfluous consideration. Reading into the Scriptures and the most prominent traditions of the Church brings to light one common element that Christian theology cannot overlook. This is that "the Christian vocation in the world is not [only] one of living an unblemished moral life to ensure one's own salvation or to give a good example to others," Monika K. Hellwig underlines. Christian theology also has the responsibility to make clear that the Christian vocation is "to live a redemptive life," something that necessitates "an alert, critical attitude leading to vigorous and creative initiatives to change the world in which we live and to bring it under the reign of God."[3] It means that theology must articulate how to honor the human being in order to honor God.

Theology can thus be seen both as an intellectual discipline as well as a guide to concrete Christian living in the world guided by faith. Both wings are necessary to make authentic theology fly. Theological reflection must have a part to play in the public transformation of society beyond individual concerns of personal piety. Pertaining to the goal of integral flourishing of every woman and man and every community, theology must be "political" and "liberating." Exclusively limiting the task of theology to the dimension of faith seeking understanding or its philosophical or speculative level alone is therefore narrow and reductionist. It risks distorting theology's essence because its other and equally important limb as faith seeking transformation of life will be severed.

---

3. Hellwig, *What Are the Theologians Saying Now?* 134.

That "the Christian vocation in the world is to work together to make radical and structural changes, especially on behalf of those who are left out"[4] comprised a theological vision highly developed by the Fathers or Doctors of the Church. They lived and wrote in the first six centuries of the Church's existence. Among them are the anonymous authors of *The Didache* (c. 70 or 90 or 120 or 150), the *Letter to Diognetus* (c. 190 or 200) and *The Shepherd of Hermas* (between 100 and 160). But there are also the writings of Clement of Rome (d. 99), Ignatius of Antioch (d. 115), Justin Martyr (c. 100–165), Origen (c. 184-254), Tertullian (c. 155-220) and Cyprian of Carthage (c. 200-258). Other important resources in this respect are the writings of Clement of Alexandria (c. 150–216), Basil the Great (c. 330–79), Ambrose of Milan (c. 333–97), John Chrysostom (c. 344–407), Jerome (c. 347–419), Augustine of Hippo (354–430), and Gregory the Great (c. 540–604).

These works theologically engage with the nature and style of civil organization, and the position they adopt is surprisingly similar. It revolves around the manner of ownership of property. The writers reflect on the actual manner of ownership of material goods in society and find it to be the controlling agent in interpersonal and social relationships. It determines the nature and structure of society. For the Doctors of the Church, the manner of ownership not only forms how the rights and dignity of some persons are perceived, but also how the order of existence itself in the world is actually shaped. The enduring legacy they have bequeathed to the Church is always to question whether the dominant system of ownership of goods facilitates compassionate human relationships as intended by God's gifting of creation to all. This applies particularly to the system of land tenure. What constitutes the structure of land distribution forms the basis of structures of ownership. This question of ownership forms the core of patristic theology on social morality.

The theological thinking of Clement, for example, with regards to economic and, therefore, socio-political organization grants the right of material self-sufficiency (*autarkeia*) to everyone. Implied here is the legitimacy of private property. Clement sees this as a necessary condition of proper and dignified self-perception of the individual person. No one should have to depend entirely on others for one's survival. But Clement does not take individual self-sufficiency as the final goal of ownership. He argues, on the contrary, that self-reliance can be justified only in the context of the self-reliance of everyone else. According to Clement's *Paedagogus*, sharing (*koinonia*) constitutes the divinely-established purpose of ownership, since material goods are God's gift to every human being. As Clement understands it, it is unworthy of anyone to boast that "I own something and I have more than enough; why should I

---

4. Hellwig, *What Are the Theologians Saying Now?* 135.

not enjoy it [alone]?" Rather, the attitude of the Christian worthy of the name should be: "I have something, why should I not share it with those in need?" In Clement's theological paradigm, just distribution of goods is what public authorities are charged to guard.

The same idea is articulated perhaps even more radically and uncompromisingly by Basil, who insists that anything superfluous that anyone owns must not be counted to belong to him or her. For Basil, inequality in material possessions subverts the right order of existence. As he puts it illustratively,

> The bread which you hold back belongs to the hungry; the coat, which you guard in your locked storage-chests, belongs to the naked; the footwear mouldering in your closet belongs to those without shoes. The silver that you keep hidden in a safe place belongs to the one in need. Thus, however many are those whom you could have provided for, so many are those whom you wrong.[5]

Essentially, patristic theology underlines the point that "Redistributing wealth [in socio-economic contexts of gross inequality] is simply an act of restitution, for the concentration of wealth in the hands of a few . . . [deprives] the poor majority of their birth right."[6] And, foreshadowing today's economic relationships, particularly in international relations, the theology of the Doctors of the Church underlines the impropriety of "charity" as a normative principle of social action to alleviate suffering. Charity is not virtuous if institutions and structures of gross injustice are preserved intact. John Chrysostom disdains the "charitable" mentality such as that which goes under the name of "aid" today because it does not address the roots of the disorder that is social injustice. For Chrysostom, the fundamental step toward Christian order is to stop corruption, "For, unless you desist from your robbery, you are not actually giving alms. Even though you should give ever so much money to the needy, if you do not desist from your fraud and robbery you shall be numbered by God among the murderers." Augustine seems to reject altogether the institution of private property, which he perceives as rather silly, considering that all human beings have comparable basic needs. "Will the rich person have two stomachs to fill because of being rich?" he mocks. The social theology of Augustine emphasizes the construction of economic equity in the human family, arguing that in the end blatant inequality in material possessions is produced by injustice and is therefore an enemy of peace. Augustine's theological approach

---

5. Migne, Patrologia Graeca, 32:1158. See also: Goodreads Incorporation, "Basil the Great," Accessed August 8, 2016. http://www.goodreads.com/quotes/672732-the-bread-which-you-hold-back-belongs-to-the-hungry

6. Avila, Ownership, 68.

is definitely not "communist" in the deterministic and atheistic Marxist sense, but it is "socialist" in the Christian understanding of the term, which is characterized by "deep concern for the well-being of workers, commitment to the equal dignity of all humans, and [provides] a *justification for state interventions in the economy* to protect losers in economic competition."[7]

Social conditions born of given historical realities necessarily play a role in contemporary theological imagination in one way or another. They also influence the forms that theological articulation takes. The Industrial Revolution of the nineteenth century was no exception.

After several centuries of scholastic theology from about the eighth century, the Christian theological style had become highly theoretical and speculative, hardly touching on real-life issues of suffering caused by poverty, hunger and oppression as a result of mal-distribution of wealth. The tendency had been to relegate these issues almost exclusively to the civil authorities. A perspective best described as withdrawal from or non-engagement with the physical world of politics and economics had developed and established itself. The Industrial Revolution was to shake that paradigm and change it profoundly. The Revolution was marked by the process of technological innovation that led to radical changes in the structures of society. The economic system now changed from feudalism based on fiefdom to mass employment of labor in manufacturing enterprises. From the feudalistic three-tier social organization of lords, vassals and fiefs there emerged a two-tier social order of industrial owners and employees.

The cruel consequences of this new system of ownership impacted consciences. The practical behavior of the owners of industry or capitalists towards their employees, the industrial workers or proletariat, formed the catalyst for novel philosophical and theological reflections on "the condition of the workers." This thinking is represented most prominently by the writings of Karl Marx and by Pope Leo XIII in his encyclical *Rerum Novarum,* "On the Condition of Labor." As a reaction against both the inhuman excesses of liberal capitalism and the totalitarian atheistic socialism proposed by Karl Marx, *Rerum Novarum* marked the beginning of a profound paradigm shift in the Christian theological imagination concerning the interaction between Church, wealth and society. The question was implicit and not framed in so many words, but it was nevertheless unmistakable: What is the place and role of the Church guided by Christian theology in this suffering of the masses? What is the responsibility of the individual Christian and the Christian community in civil society, acting under the ethical imperative of the Gospel?

---

7. Massaro, "Christian Socialism," 212.

Christian Socialists in the United States, such as Washington Gladden and Walter Rauschenbusch with their "Social Gospel Movement" in the early twentieth century, exemplified the endeavor of applying Gospel values concretely to social issues. At about the same time, some prominent theologians like Reinhold Niebuhr, Karl Barth, and Paul Tillich mirrored the same concern. Niebuhr's attempt "to mediate between biblical faith and social issues, between religion and power politics, as well as between self-transcendent spirit and finite nature within the human constitution reflected his prophetic perspective on the social Gospel."[8]

On a more institutional and official level, apart from the 1971 second Ordinary General Assembly of the Synod of Bishops in the Catholic Church, the World Council of Churches (WCC) established the Justice, Peace and Integrity of Creation Commission (JPIC) in Vancouver, Canada, in 1983 with the specific Mission Statement "To analyze and reflect on justice, peace, and creation in their interrelatedness, to promote values and practices that make for a culture of solidarity with young people, women, Indigenous Peoples, and racially oppressed people."[9]

Earlier in 1971, Pope Paul VI had spelt out at great length this theological approach in a letter called *Octogesima Adeveniens* addressed to Cardinal Maurice Roy, President of the Council of the Laity and of the Pontifical Commission of Justice and Peace in Rome. Commemorating the 80th anniversary of *Rerum Novarum,* the Pope affirmed that it behooves local Christian communities "to analyze with objectivity the situation which is proper to their own country," and "to discern the options and commitments which are called for in order to bring about the social, political and economic changes seen in many cases to be urgently needed" (*Octogesima Adeveniens,* no. 4). Nevertheless, formal theology must play a role in the process, he wrote, explaining that theological reflection must accompany and inspire Christian communities by confronting practical issues with the demands of the Gospel, without pretending to offer final or definitive solutions (no. 42).

Later in the twentieth century there emerged new theological approaches that, more explicitly and practically than before, put emphasis not only on orthodoxy, or correct belief, but also equally on orthopraxis, or correct action. It is a theology that insists that for faith in Jesus the Christ to be authentic, the two must go together. It confesses that it cannot avoid addressing ideologies

---

8 "Reinhold Niebuhr." In New World Encyclopedia. Accessed May 20, 2016. http://www.newworldencyclopedia.org/entry/Reinhold_Niebuhr. For a detailed study of Christian Socialism in general, see Cort, *Christian Socialism.*

9. The Forum on Religion and Ecology at Yale, "World Council of Churches (WCC) Justice, Peace, and Creation (JPC)," fore.yale.edu/, accessed March 15, 2016. http://fore.yale.edu/religion/christianity/projects/wcc_jpc/.

and practices that privilege some people at the expense of others. It insists further that while cultures must be continually purified by the Gospel of Christ, they must be respected in the evangelization process because it is in culture that God's self-revelation is intuited. These are the theologies of liberation and inculturation. As far as the Gospel of Christ is concerned there is no place in social relationships for toleration of oppression of human beings or for imperialism in intercultural relations. All human beings share equal dignity and should be treated as such; no single culture has precedence above others because any and every culture can be a vehicle of the Good News of Christ.

On account of the process of globalization and the flow of political, economic and information power, systems and structures of economic inequality have spread throughout the world. The yawning gap between the haves and the have-nots, the rich and the poor, is evident internationally. In Africa, Asia and Latin America, this is a theological issue because it causes enormous suffering on the part of the vast majority of the hemisphere's population. Pushed to the periphery of human society, and actually excluded from access to the proper enjoyment of the goods of creation, they experience great suffering. Different shades of Liberation and Inculturation Theology now explicitly address these issues of economic and cultural oppression, marginalization, and exclusion of some people from the circle of human rights and dignity.

Among theologians of the North, Political Theology also developed in the North in the latter part of the twentieth century to explore the notion of the suffering or "crucified" God in the faces of the poor. Among the representatives of this theological genre were Jürgen Moltmann and Johann Baptist Metz. What political theologians have done is to take seriously into account and apply in practical terms Jesus' manifesto of his own mission on earth as earlier prophesied by Isaiah (61:1) and cited by Jesus himself (Luke 4:18–19). It is not possible to "spiritualize" this mandate in any credible way by arguing that it has nothing to do with practical economics or politics. Though it is true that the point of the manifesto is not primarily to push through or impose one particular political ideology over any other, it nevertheless does provide a horizon. The point of the manifesto, as Pope Paul VI explained in *Octogesima Adveniens* (no. 43) is to emphasize "the need to establish greater justice in the sharing of goods, both within national communities and on the international level."

This is what Pope Francis has also argued for, insisting that believers and non-believers should be united in the conviction that "the earth is essentially a shared inheritance, whose fruits are meant to benefit everyone." For followers of Jesus Christ, the implications of this shared conviction bear a direct political, economic, and social agenda. Any national or international political program that attempts to legitimize a "model of distribution, where a minority believes that it has the right to consume in a way which can never be universalized" or applied to all, especially "the least of these" (Matt 25:40), is intrinsically sinful. It needs to be overhauled. Any economic ideology that elevates any form of private ownership of property to an "absolute or inviolable" principle goes against a central value of the long-standing tradition of sharing of the Christian faith. It must be rejected. Any social structure that disregards the norm of human equity in the sense that the "rich and the poor have equal dignity," is innately flawed. It must be transformed (see *Laudato Si*, no. 54, 94). What it means in practical terms is that everyone, especially the very poor, "has a natural right to possess a reasonable allotment of land where he can establish his home, work for subsistence of his family and a secure life." Pope Francis explains that "This right must be guaranteed so that its exercise is not illusory but real. That means that apart from the ownership of property, rural people must have access to means of technical education, credit, insurance, and markets" (no. 94).

The historical figures who embodied best the practical demands of theology and who demonstrated starkly the tension between theology and social transformation were the Hebrew prophets. They placed theological conviction squarely in the public square. Their stance has implications and should be paradigmatic for any subsequent theological process. Their proclamations were not personal initiatives but an imperative from God. The Hebrew prophets never tired of pointing out that they were merely God's mouthpieces and that, therefore, they cannot escape from the dangerous responsibility, much as they might prefer to do so. There have been modern and contemporary prophets of the same kind, some of whom paid for it with their lives. Their message, like that of the ancient prophets has been founded on the imperative: "This is what the Lord says."

Indeed, God has not left himself without witnesses in every nation and at all times. Today, there are people who, whether explicitly professing the Christian faith or not, have nevertheless demonstrated deep spirituality that is not only personal and private, but one that engages with contemporary, public situations. It is an integral spirituality that calls people to be and do what the Lord says and wants of them. These are individuals and groups who, very closely by their actions, attend to the practical requirements of the Beatitudes (Matt 5:3–11) and of human relationships, thereby earning them the designation of "blessed" in God's eyes (Matt 25:31–46). Examples in the eyes of many include Nelson Mandela and Bishop Desmond Tutu from South Africa. The former witnessed by defending the human rights and dignity of all persons. Bishop Tutu joined hands with Mandela in defending the image of the Creator God in every person. Both were willing and ready to sacrifice their very lives for this goal. Martin Luther King in the United States and Bishop Oscar Romero in El Salvador form another pair. They literally paid with their lives for putting theology in the public realm. In a similar line and for the same end, contemporary organizations such as Médecins Sans Frontières (Doctors without Borders) must also be included in the list. There are other less famous witnesses of the divine will, but it is not fame but the public witness of the Gospel that matters most in the form of a theology that actively strives for justice.

There have been periods in the history of the Church when theology tried to ignore its "social" and "public" responsibility. It embraced the dualistic Manichaean view of the world as justification for such a stance. It thought that since politics and economics dealt with material things, which it deemed evil, they did not constitute theology's responsibility, which it perceived as exclusively "spiritual." But the human person is an indivisible whole, a composite of matter and Spirit. This theological view was therefore found to be untenable; in fact, it often only served to sustain structural injustice and oppression. Put under the scrutiny of the Gospel, it could not endure. Contemporary theology, inspired by scriptural and Patristic consciousness of the social implications of the Christian faith and theology, has rediscovered its public role. Since Vatican II, it has become clear that it is incumbent on theology to demonstrate the way toward God's reign by fulfilling the demands of justice, reconciliation and peace.

Chapter 12

Models of Governance for Development in Africa

GOOD GOVERNANCE AND DEVELOPMENT cannot be separated. As a rule, good governance facilitates holistic human development, whereas bad governance obstructs growth. The challenge that faces the African continent in this respect is for African nations to construct models of governance that address the "underdevelopment" malaise. What are some of the ways of dealing with and changing the situation of underdevelopment in Africa? Catholic theology has a role to play in this endeavor under the guidance of the Social Teaching of the Church (STC).[1]

For well over a century now, the Catholic Church has promoted a consistent, broad, and comprehensive understanding of development or progress as part of its social thought. This was already implicit in the seminal letter of Pope Leo XIII's *Rerum Novarum* of 1891. This letter launched the Catholic Church's official reflection on social issues into modern times. Appropriately, this tradition is known as the Social Teaching of the Church (STC). Since the end of the nineteenth century, it has been taken up, carried on, and expanded with more and more precision and clarity by subsequent Popes, especially Pope Pius XI (1922–39) and Pope John XXIII (1958–63). But it is particularly Pope Paul VI (1963–78) who crystallized the meaning of development for the least developed countries in his letter *Populorum Progressio* of 1967.

Pope Paul VI argues in the letter that "authentic" development must be "integral." He maintains that development is first of all development of people,

---
1. For example, see Brady, *Essential Catholic Social Thought*.

of human beings, not things. He argues further that if development or progress does not involve the whole person and all persons, it cannot be authentic but illusory and false. The Pope's central point is, therefore, that the kind of development that does not embrace the whole person, body and soul, and all human beings in the same way, whoever and wherever they are, is anything but genuine. True development must move people "from less human conditions to those which are more human." "Development" is internally corrupted and does not deserve the name, from the Christian point of view, if it fails to do this. It is pseudo-development and already contains the seeds of its own destruction. This is because it does not satisfy the three essential conditions that guarantee the authenticity of the type of progress that is human and comprehensive: namely, integration of the person or group of persons first with themselves, with others, and with God.

The deliberations of Vatican II emphasize this definition, as does Pope John Paul II's reflections on the social question during his long and prolific pontificate (1978–2005). The Roman Synods dealing with the social question since 1965 include the same trend of thought, as do various progressive regional and national Episcopal Conferences as well as various pronouncements by individual bishops. Pope Benedict XVI in his 2009 letter *Caritas in Veritate*, "Charity in Truth," (no. 18) has re-articulated Pope Paul VI's insights on authentic development most clearly set forth in the latter's landmark encyclical, *Populorum Progressio*. This consistent understanding of development in the Church's thought, must form the basis and reference point of any discussion on the Catholic theological view of human progress. It leads to an appreciation of the necessary relationship between governance and development.

According to the STC, there are four essential components of genuine development which can be grouped into two broad categories:

a. the material aspect, and
b. the transcendental or, according to some, spiritual aspect.

Pope Benedict XVI in *Caritas in Veritate* (no. 18) describes the one as belonging to the "natural plane" and the other to the "supernatural plane" of human development. There is no question of artificially separating or prioritizing them in a so-called order of importance, and Pope Benedict XVI certainly does not do so. Both are equally important, each being intrinsically connected to the other. This interconnection is evident by considering their various components.

In the material aspect of development, the components include politics and economics. Politics involves the actual or prospective exercise of authority or control over a population of people. A simple definition of politics is that it is the art, science, method, or system of management of people. But governance cannot be separated from economics. Political authority also involves in large measure supervision over what, how and where material goods are obtained, processed, divided and consumed—in other words, economics. No government can escape from this task, which pertains to its responsibility of safeguarding the common good and of maintaining law and order. It is the task of safeguarding fundamental human rights.

Articulated most prominently in the United Nations' Universal Declaration of Human Rights of 1948, the understanding of basic human rights has been expanded since then with reference to socio-cultural rights. Because human rights are at the center of Christian theological anthropology, models of managing and directing the political and social aspects of society are similarly central to the theological view of development. Human rights entail the sense of progress from less to more human conditions. At this level, we are talking about the individual person's or a human group's right relationship with others and the created order.

But there is also the equally important transcendental aspect of development that is often overlooked in simple definitions of the notion. Its components include moral and spiritual elements of progress. These have to do with a person's or group's relationship with self and God or the Transcendent. Whereas the material elements have to do mostly with visible, scientifically verifiable aspects of human life, including the distribution of resources in the form of infrastructure—roads, schools, hospitals, and so on—the transcendental aspects of development cannot be so empirically evaluated or directly managed. Yet, the transcendental relies also on the material organization of society, and the right ordering of society if founded on transcendental principles.

For lack of a better expression, one might say that the transcendental category of development and its components are in the "subjective" realm. They are concerned with the spirit and the psyche of the human person both as an individual and as society. Socially, they are the foundation of culture. They involve such attitudes and dispositions as concern and care for others (that is, charity, love, compassion, mercy, at the spiritual level), a sense of justice (at the moral or ethical level), and internal peace, freedom, and contentment, happiness, tolerance, and temperance (at the psychical-spiritual level). Although it has to be said once more that these are internal virtues which cannot be directly managed or controlled by some external authority, they have as much to do with authentic development, as understood by the STC, as the material components. It makes sense, therefore, to affirm with regards to religion that it cannot be fully appreciated and appropriated until it becomes a culture.

Similarly, material development is unfulfilling until it is assimilated into the transcendental, spiritual culture.

The position of the STC is that if it is to be true human progress, material progress must be able to bring about transcendental progress in the person and society. According to the STC, it is the presence and influence of the transcendental in the human person and in society as a whole that makes material progress meaningful and satisfying. Transcendental development gives material progress human meaning. It humanizes an otherwise merely mechanical process. The argument in concrete terms is that roads, schools, hospitals, and technology, which are the external realm and immediate concern of governance, are instruments of true development only if they expand the dignity—that is, the freedom, contentment, and happiness—of each and all persons in society. This is the internal realm or spirituality and morality of progress. To the extent that the material aspect of development fails to impact the transcendental on the one hand, and the transcendental fails to give direction to the material on the other, to the same extent must development be seen as inadequate. In other words, to the point that governance lacks the spirit of justice, fairness, compassion, and tolerance, to that same extent can it not facilitate true development. The correlation is mutual and essential in the view of the STC. It involves the understanding of the social economy on the one hand, and that of the dignity of the human person on the other.

According to the STC, the economy must serve the human person.[2] Three main principles are involved in this. Economic activity in all of its dimensions must serve the dignity of each person, cater for the fundamental equality of all, and acknowledge concretely every person's inalienable rights to life and dignity. With regard to its activities the economy must always take the person as subject, attend to the common good under the ideals of justice and charity, and must be tempered by concern for the survival of the earth.

From all of this, the role of governance does not lie in the multiplication and betterment of material goods alone. Another question that must always be asked is: whom do they serve? Material development must be sensitive to the increase and improvement of human possibilities for dignity and internal and social freedom. It must forge human solidarity in terms of a widening sense of satisfaction and happiness because of the availability and accessibility of material goods to as wide a circle of the population as possible. Central to the expansion of freedom is the guarantee of freedom of belief, religion, and information. Articles 18 and 19 of the Universal Declaration of Human Rights address these freedoms and rights. Pope Benedict XVI in *Caritas in Veritate* (no. 18) speaks about the importance of religion in the process of

---

2. See Collins and Wright, *The Moral Measure of the Economy*.

development, remarking that "when God is eclipsed, our ability to recognize the natural order, purpose and the 'good' [of development] begins to wane."

The combination of the two dimensions of integral development is what is lacking in African models of governance. But what kind of models of governance are in place in Africa today? Do they fulfill the requirements for integral development as spelled out in the STC? Have the material and transcendental categories of development in all their components been adequately integrated half a century after political independence?

Four models of governance may be distinguished across the continent during this period: the single-party mass movements; one-person dictatorships; failing or failed states; and fledgling democracies. Incidentally, these developments have been chronological, more or less in that order. But, first of all, why did they emerge?

Peace Studies scholars Aquiline Tarimo and Paulin Manwelo identify three major causes of the African governance malaise. They argue that, first there has been a rapid and unfortunate "disintegration of value systems" in Africa, which has not augured well for imagination for homegrown political ideologies. This has led, secondly, to a "deterioration of political institutions," whether indigenous or imported. Thirdly, the mindless "scramble for inadequate resources" has led to an inevitable moral or ethical deterioration of both leaders and citizens, thus preventing the economy from being at the service of the human person and the common good.[3]

It has been argued that perhaps the worst damage the colonial system did to the African continent was not the rape of the economic and human resources in the form of material exploitation and slavery. Ngugi wa Thiong'o is convinced that these cannot compare to the "colonization of the mind" that African people were subjected to. This entailed the alienation of the people from their roots and their culture which was achieved through a form of alienating education and religion. This process was intended to turn Africans into unreflective imitators of foreign values. Political governance was particularly hit by this situation. Since independence, most leaders have been merely eager to step into the shoes of the departing colonial masters, so that to govern and lead has been to act like the latter. In a sense the colonial masters have never left; they have merely changed masks. This has not brought any real development, in the sense of respect for persons and attention to the common good. Because "development theories" in Africa have had no foundation in cultural values, the resultant situation in the population has been "identity crisis, lack

---

3. Tarimo and Manwelo, *African Peacemaking and Governance*, 20–28.

of self-confidence, and inefficiency," sinking many "into the cloud of confusion, frustration, and disorder."[4]

Thus, "the transfer of power from colonialism [into African hands] became a transfer of crisis." In the purely political sphere, except for only a few, the leaders of the nationalist movement to whom powers of government were handed over on Independence Day had little or no expertise in the details of governance. In fact, the colonial authorities had made sure to undermine or eliminate anyone who showed any kind of endowment in this area. Consequently, at independence, there was generally no adequate cadre of people capable enough of handling matters of state with the dedication, imagination, impartiality, efficiency, and proficiency that functional democratic dispensations require. As an extreme but by no means exceptional example, in five centuries of Portuguese presence in parts of Africa (1471–1971), only twenty-five Africans had been educated to professional and technical level! The situation was not very much different in the French and English colonies, with only the duration of colonial stay being shorter. At any rate, the colonial intention of providing any kind of education was to assimilate the African into the mentality of the colonial masters, thus creating white people in black skins.

The most conspicuous characteristic of governance at every level in Africa soon revealed itself to be crass incompetence, evidenced by mindless authoritarianism, nepotism, tribalism, and repression. Furthermore, afraid of losing grip on power, the new elites suppressed traditional governing systems. They were either incapable or unwilling to learn from indigenous systems of governance in terms of methods for community cohesion and resource distribution to serve the human person and the common good. In general, there was no innovative political theory to inspire a transformative human-centered social, economic, and political movement.

In the economic and social spheres, the colonial system had left no infrastructure to speak of. Huge territories had no railway lines, no highways, a few secondary schools, no major hospitals, and no universities. Whatever "roads" existed were intended to facilitate the transfer of raw materials from inland to the coast, from where they were shipped to the colonial metropolises. This was indeed a "transfer of crisis" for it guaranteed the economic underdevelopment of the people. Obviously, it led to popular dissatisfaction with the postcolonial regimes in a very short period of time.

In several African countries, the most important resource not only for economic development but also survival is land, but land ownership is concentrated in the hands of a few. Some of these are foreign absentee landlords. Contrary to former indigenous political-economic and social arrangements,

---

4. Tarimo and Manwelo, *African Peacemaking and Governance*, 11.

many of the citizens in these countries do not own land. They had been displaced and forced to be squatters on land which had been theirs to begin with, but which the colonial settlers alienated from them. This situation has haunted many African governments for a long time, and very few steps have been taken to change it. Where something has been tried, it has been bungled by incompetence, nepotism and other forms of corruption.

In Africa, the person or group that owns the land controls the wealth of the nation. Thus internally—and externally—fuelled wars are being waged in all parts of the continent for control of mineral—or oil-rich areas. The DRC, Sierra Leone, Liberia, the Niger Delta of Nigeria, and South Sudan have all gone through this. The scramble for land has also been a source of major corruption scandals all over the continent. Governments have been bribed into making major and unjustifiable concessions to foreign companies for land accession, mining, logging, hunting, agricultural or industrial exploitation, and so on, with little or no benefit to the people of the countries or regions concerned. One notorious example is Shell's activities in the Niger Delta region of Nigeria. A protestor against such unconscionable exploitation and pollution by Shell, namely, Ken Saro-Wiwa, was persecuted and executed by his own government.

Models of governance since independence in Africa have fallen broadly within this general political, economic and social malaise. The single-party mass movement under a charismatic leader was the model favored immediately following independence. It was a euphoric period in these years. There had been a common enemy for everyone to fight against only a short time previously, namely colonialism with its oppression, discrimination and degradation of the natives. After independence, the feeling of "us against them" lingered on, somehow fuelled by the Cold War at its height at this time. The former colonial masters from the western bloc were too ready to interfere in subtle and not-too subtle ways in the decision of their ex-colonial territories, especially if these leaned towards the East. To prevent the spread of communism seemed to be their all-encompassing mission.

Unfortunately, the charismatic founding fathers of the new African nations did not want to relinquish power. They stayed at the helm for an inordinately long time. Nevertheless, two remarkable things must be mentioned about this period. First, for the most part, there was a general feeling of contentment and hope among the people. Having recently thrown down the yoke of colonialism, hope for freedom ensued. People hoped that their material lot would eventually change for the better. It is possible to interpret this as an expression at that time of transcendental development, where a feeling of self-identity, equality, dignity and even happiness permeated people's consciousness. On account of the political freedom they had recently obtained, people felt they "were more" even if they did not actually "have more."

Interestingly, for a handful of countries, this marks the only politically imaginative and creative period in terms of serious indigenous models of governance in the history of post-colonial Africa. There were some very constructive ideologies thought up by several founding fathers, intended to put into effect the principles of human dignity and the social economy. For example, Kwame Nkrumah's "Conscientism" (Ghana), Leopold Sedar Senghor's "Negritude" (Senegal), Kenneth Kaunda's "Humanism" (Zambia), or Julius K. Nyerere's "Ujamaa" (Tanzania). Both Pope Paul VI's *Populorum Progressio* and Nyerere's "The Arusha Declaration," the document outlining the principles of political, economic and social governance in Tanzania, were published in 1967. Despite their many shortcomings, the original political attempts founded on African values were remarkable and have not been replicated since. Some of the initiatives, like Nyerere's Ujamaa, reflected solid Christian principles.

Eventually, the people were disenchanted with charisma without food in the granaries, with ideology without medicine in the dispensaries, or fuel at petrol stations, or salaries for schoolteachers, or goods in the stores. They were also unhappy with the increasing tyranny of the one-party system, with its intolerance of variety of political views, the blatant promotion of ethnic patronage systems, the shameless cultivation of a personality cult, and the growing abuse of power by leaders, shown in frequent instances of detentions without trial. One after another, several founding fathers were violently overthrown in the late 1960s and early 1970s. It began, ominously, with Ghana, which had been the first country in sub-Sahara Africa to gain independence in 1957. It is as though the toppling and exiling of Kwame Nkrumah set in motion something of a domino effect around the continent. What replaced the founding regimes were in most cases one-man military dictatorships. Even in the few countries where, as in Kenya, the first president died a natural death still in power, what succeeded them were dictatorships.

These dictatorial regimes became the most brutal and tyrannical imaginable. The names of Idi Amin Dada (Uganda), Jean-Bedel Bokassa (Central African Republic), Mathieu Kerekou (Benin), Mobutu Sese Seko (Congo), or Samuel Doe and Charles Taylor (Liberia) easily come to mind. The distinguishing mark of these and other regimes during this time across the continent was everything that the STC would disprove of: despotism. Constitutions were summarily suspended or eliminated, and no rule of law existed. There was no conception of human rights or any idea of the common good. Anybody's life was expendable to protect the survival of the regime.

Marking these regimes were repression, extrajudicial killings and disappearances, rampant corruption and nepotism, ethnic persecution, and human rights abuses, rape, intimidation, intrigue, impunity, and terror. There were weak or no working public institutions. What prevailed was contempt for the rule of law, the use of the army to suppress dissent, and systematic intellectual repression. Makerere University, the premier academic institution in the whole of the Eastern African region was literally shattered under Amin, with many of its intellectual leading lights either assassinated or forced into exile. Ali Mazrui under the regime of Idi Amin Dada, Ngugi wa Thiong'o under the regime of Daniel arap Moi, and Wole Soyinka, the first African Nobel Laureate for Literature (1986), under the regime of General Sani Abacha all suffered exile. In Liberia in 1982, President Samuel Doe issued Decree 2A "banning all academic activities that 'directly or indirectly impinge, interfere with or cast aspersion upon the activities, programs or policies of the People's Redemption Council [i.e. his junta].'"[5] Here as elsewhere in African institutions of higher learning during these regimes, there was general harassment of staff and students. Academic freedom, freedom of thought and expression, or anything similar, save the "freedom" of cheering the leader, was taboo.

These rulers were generally ruthless. For example, while the "Lion Warrior, Savior of the Nation, Supreme Combatant" (Mobutu) was an accomplished Machiavellian, criminal performer, the "Emperor of the Central African Republic" (Bokassa), and "Field Marshall," "White Man's Burden" [the "Butcher of Uganda"] (Amin) were cruel buffoons. It is tragic that in spite of all of this, the Organization of African Unity (OAU, now African Union or AU) conceded its chairmanship to Amin in 1975. This move also blocked his censure for human rights abuses by the United Nations.

It is easy to see from this that development as respect for human dignity and the common good was lost in this decade for Africa. Apart from devising machinations for their own survival, the dictators were not interested in their countries or their people. The Democratic Republic of Congo and Somalia, among others, are until now reaping the consequences of the seeds sown then, particularly with regard to ethnic tension and lack of a cohesive sense of nationhood. What governed politics and economics was the principle of "It's Our Turn to Eat."

There being scarcely any genuine political organization during the years of the one-strongman rule, when he fell off the scene, the resultant situation was anarchy and chaos. It is a situation characterized by rape, abduction of children as sex-slaves and soldiers, warlords, and other nefarious activities. But anarchy and chaos are the distinctive marks of a failing or

---

5. Berkley, *Graves Are Not Yet Full*, 33.

failed state, the symptoms of the failure depending on the degree of absence or disregard for law and order. Failed states are ungovernable and very difficult to stabilize. Suffering, destruction, and death are the daily lot of the people. No meaningful development project can take place. Conscience, and therefore spiritual growth, is stunted so that neither human life nor respect for creation counts for anything. In a failed state, an unscrupulous foreign company can easily dump tons of toxic waste in the middle of a city, killing or injuring untold numbers of people and get away with it. What happened in Abidjan, Cote d'Ivoire, in 2006 is an instance. Trafigura, a Texas, USA-owned company, shipped and dumped 500 tons of toxic waste in unsecured public dumps and along roads in populated areas in Abidjan, claiming it was "dirty water." Upwards of 100,000 people are reported to have been affected by the fumes from the waste. Among them many died. The Netherlands had refused to accept this waste for storage because the company would not pay the amount necessary for it.

A classic example of a failed state is, of course, Somalia after the ouster of Mohammed Siad Barre in 1991. Somalia has been in a state of chaos ever since, despite numerous efforts by the international community to stabilize it. Not surprisingly, criminal elements find a haven there, including Al-Qaeda group, Islamic State militants, kidnappers, and sea pirates. These states are also referred to as "rogue states" due to absence of rule of law in their international relations. But Somalia has not been unique in this category in Africa. Liberia after Samuel Doe was for a time another example. Consider further the political, economic and social situation of some of the countries of the Great Lakes region for a good picture of failing states. The Democratic Republic of Congo is the case of choice in this region. But Rwanda had been in a similar situation before President Paul Kagame seized the reins of power in 1994. Neighboring Burundi is not out of the woods yet with regard to this crisis.

In the midst of an abysmal picture such as this, there are two or three examples in the continent where attempts at some degree of good governance are recorded. Mentioned frequently are Ghana, Botswana, and post-apartheid South Africa. Since independence, Botswana, for example, has been able to hold several elections that were comparatively sufficiently transparent, free and fair, enabling power at the highest levels to devolve without major violence and in accordance with the constitution of the country. Botswana has also been able to establish credentials of a degree of economic democracy, an essential element toward the recognition of the dignity of the person as advocated by the STC.

Good examples of democratic governance though these nations may be, they may be standing on sand. They have established their structures by almost totally imitating western systems of "democracy," without appropriating the concept and inculturating it in the African reality. This type of democracy remains a potted plant, with roots in foreign soil. There is hardly African imagination here. In other words, there is little evidence that the culture and political systems of their own people have contributed significantly to the construction of these structures. But if authentic development must take into account a people's dignity, that is, its identity, this must be done. There needs to be consideration about models of governance in Africa that support authentic development.

There are three elements necessary for processes of governance that will answer to the aspirations of the African people to progress as fully integrated persons. These are democracy, Africanity, and rootedness. Democracy seems to be the best form of governance. What precisely is democracy? Where Africa is concerned, this is not an idle question, especially when, again for lack of local political imagination, certain models of democracy are being forced upon African societies as the only feasible ones. What does "government of the people, by the people, for the people" imply in concrete African circumstances? Great Britain, The Netherlands, Belgium are constitutional monarchies, yet they are democracies. France, Germany, and the US are republics, but also democracies. Is it because these entities have multiple political parties and hold periodical elections that they qualify as such?

While it is all this, democracy is much more. True democracy is founded on an "attitude of mind" or rather a moral conviction, perhaps best expressed by Lincoln in the sentiment: "As I would not be a slave, so I would not be a master. This expresses my idea of democracy." Lincoln argued that "Whatever differs from this, to the extent of the difference, is no democracy." Again, he asserted in the same vein that "those who deny freedom to others, deserve it not for themselves; and, under a just God, cannot long retain it."[6]

What is the meaning of this sentiment for democracy? It means that the democratic conviction must be based not only on outward manifestations in the form of political parties, electoral campaigns, and casting of the ballot. Important as these are as expressions of democracy, what forms democracy's vital foundation is the prior belief in the equality and dignity of every human being, every member of society. In a true democracy, this must be demonstrated in practical terms. To the extent that this belief is lacking, to the same extent does talk of democracy or the social motions of the same remain a veneer for tyranny.

Governance as exercise of authority or control involves a system of meanings, values, goals, and means to achieve them. In terms of Africanity,

6. Basler, *Collected Works*, 376, 532.

what is the meaning of the human person and society? What values does a given African society espouse for itself and in relation to those other societies with which it inevitably must come into contact? Based on these meanings and values, what are the goals desired in the short and long run? Crucially, what are the means to be employed to achieve the goals? To construct models of governance suitable for Africa, African nations must ask and seek contextual answers to these questions for themselves.

Africa cannot afford to import foreign models wholesale however successful they have been elsewhere. But this has been the case up to now. The post-independence political history of Africa shows how this can be absolutely dysfunctional. Uncritical imitation is not able to take into serious account the meanings and values of African societies, which the means employed and goals envisaged in governance must serve. African imagination is fundamental to the task of constructing appropriate models of governance for authentic, holistic development models, which would take into serious account the principles and aspirations of democracy in Africa. "It does not seem likely that true liberation is possible without rediscovering deep-rooted cultural traditions," Tarimo and Manwelo argue. "In order to promote acceptable and effective models that could enforce human rights and democratic ideals, it is necessary to encourage Africans to believe in themselves by developing an attitude of self-esteem that requires them to identify themselves with their own cultures."[7]

Finally, there is the related element of rootedness, the sense of history and tradition. There are cynics, of course, who doubt the distinctiveness of African culture and its possible contribution to models of governance in the continent. They would erode the African people's "self-esteem . . . to identify themselves with their own cultures." Yet, like any other civilization, African societies were organized under the guidance of great human values, on the one hand, but also were liable to ignore or abuse them. In other words, they had magnanimity of vision but limitations in practice. The challenge for contemporary governance in Africa is to gradually capture the vision of indigenous Africa while as much as possible eliminating its limitations.

Beset with many problems about governance, some have been tempted to "give up on Africa." There are many reasons, however, to trust in the resilience of the continent and its peoples. There is reason to believe that Africa can rise up and put flesh onto its best aspirations for governance. The spirit that preserved it through the trials of the slave trade, colonialism, and imperialism so that it emerged with its culture not totally vanquished, is the same spirit that can see it rise from what seems like a state of hopelessness. Looking

---

7. Tarimo and Manwelo, *African Peacemaking and Governance*, 13.

around many African countries, one notices that African peoples at the grassroots are gaining the awareness that they must take governance in their own hands, for their own welfare. There are hopeful indications throughout the continent that this popular movement is unstoppable.

Chapter 13

African Cultural Notions of Leadership

IN THEIR BOOK *Worlds of Power: Religious Thought and Political Practice in Africa,* Stephen Ellis and Gerrie ter Haar focus on the influence African indigenous philosophy and spirituality has on practical political leadership here. It should not be difficult for anyone familiar with leadership in African societies to make the link between the two. In fact, the distinction between them may even be redundant as leadership roles in both state and Church or Mosque are fundamentally seen in Africa through the same conceptual lenses. The philosophy and spirituality that inform civil conceptions and practices of leadership are not much different from those that inform notions and practices of leadership in the religious sphere, contemporary disclaimers notwithstanding.

What is at issue is the destructive dualism that influences perceptions and the exercise of leadership in contemporary Africa. At one level, there is the fundamental communal pull of expectations and demands from indigenous perceptions among leaders and subjects alike, that one's immediate community's interests come first and override all other considerations in the exercise of leadership. In spite of frequent public statements by leaders and a general vague feeling from the public that African societies should conform to "modern" methods and expectations of leadership, the communal principle with all its cultural implications is the deeper and controlling understanding of leadership among the majority of African populations.

This socio-religious philosophy of "community" lies at the root of ubiquitous and often questionable practices in the exercise of leadership in Africa today, practices that are frequently destructive of the homogeneity of the modern wider national community. These include nepotism and its larger manifestations of clan-ism and tribalism, expressed with different nuances depending on locality and circumstances. Although often explained in too simplistic terms that these phenomena evoke in contemporary ears, they are born of rather complex socio-religious expectations and demands: a leader's primary responsibility is to guard the interests of "his or her own people" by ensuring that they enjoy favored status and prosperity in the wider society. This is both a personal and community expectation. Paradoxically and to complicate matters even further, not only the particular leader's own community, but other communities outside the particular circle of the leader expect the same of him or her as a moral or ethical duty. This is the African leader's dilemma and burden.

The situation is much more complex today. In the past, the traditional leader was obliged to share public resources with a relatively small circle of relatives and friends. Today, on the contrary, the circle of expectant receivers is much wider. With contemporary democratic processes of elections, the leader must share with all those who voted for him or her. The elected leader must "pay back," as it were, by sharing with all of the electorates, by giving remuneration to them from public coffers, or offering preferential treatment to anyone who contributed to the leader's success.

In a sense, therefore, African leaders are not only perpetrators but are also in fact victims of the system. Through the system of unchecked cultural expectations, subjects compel their leaders to abuse public resources and trust. A case in point is that of two hypothetical gentlemen, Kamau and Macharia. At some point in time both Kamau and Macharia may be elected Members of Parliament by their respective constituencies. If Kamau manages to build a big house and to buy an expensive car within a short time of his election whereas Macharia does not, Kamau will be praised as a "good worker" irrespective of how he came about the money. On the contrary, Macharia will be despised as a "do-nothing" MP even by his own electorate. People will in fact encourage Kamau to "continue working" in the same way he has done. It seems that if Macharia lacks firm moral convictions, he might sooner rather than later succumb to Kamau's image and thus become a victim of his electorate's expectations.

Michela Wrong addresses a recent situation in Kenya, taking as a case study the problems that the country's former Anticorruption Chief, John Githongo, faced for trying to implement a different view of leadership.[1] The censure Githongo faced from his own community and its top leadership in

---

1. Wrong, *It's Our Turn to Eat.*

government illustrates the above assertion. And it applies to most sub-Saharan African states. The differences among them are of degree, not of substance. Consider as further examples recent situations of civil conflicts in Liberia, Rwanda, Burundi, Somalia, Sudan and South Sudan. In some areas, conflicts may be aggravated by religious or other differences in addition to the narrowly conceived sharing principle. However, at the end of the day, all of these situations are nepotistic; they arise from the philosophy of "it's our turn to eat" in the sense of circulating economic benefits and social status and influence based on parochial ethnicity.

Githongo's case in Kenya exemplifies the other level of the predicament of debilitating dualism in African conceptions and practices of leadership. It involves the very real and serious disconnect between "naturally" infused cultural emotions or sensitivities by nurture (culturally ingrained perceptions of leadership) on the one hand. On the other hand, there are the constructed models and modes of leadership promoted by rational knowledge and encouraged by modern school systems (modern education) and current global political practices and expectations. The two are not completely separate from each other in African exercises of leadership. There is, and has always been, a measure of interplay between them. African indigenous societies did not live in isolation as islands totally separate from one another and the outside world. They communicated and influenced one another. It is only that today the speed and levels of interaction are quicker and larger. But it is precisely here, in the relationship between the so-called "traditional" and the so-called "modern" that the issue is. The influence of tradition on the modern African leader does not mean simply a return to the past. Neither does the influence of modernity necessarily mean a complete rejection of indigenous heritage. What the process involves, or should involve, is rather a reconfiguration of the past in the context of modern times or, in other words, an interpretation of indigenous values for the present. Thus, leadership hermeneutics in Africa must try to figure out:

- How much interplay there is between the intuitive and rationally learned aspects of leadership;
- Whether this relationship is recognized and acknowledged by and enshrined in systems/syllabi of educational and leadership formation in the continent; and
- How educational institutions in Africa look at and advance the positive aspects of the encounter between the indigenous and modern systems and minimize the negative elements.

The oft-repeated argument that all of us live in the "modern" world is right, but it should be clear that the claim that old African traditions are all dead or dying is wishful thinking, particularly with regard to African leadership perceptions. It does not coincide with the reality on the ground, especially in the spiritual realm which is a key force in perceptions and exercise of leadership in Africa. "The African bush may be burning, but the roots are alive," as Benezet Bujo observes. The influence of African traditional culture is present in a rapidly changing world. The view of Ellis and ter Haar is that "religious ideas" are at the root of popular perception of leadership and the world in general in Africa. This has been overlooked or disregarded in many analyses because in relation to politics and economics, religion has been considered mainly in terms of its institutional forms instead of its central function as a giver of meaning or as a foundational system of looking at, interpreting, and understanding reality. But it is this sense that is at work in African leadership conceptions, whether religious or secular.

In a well-argued essay called "Perseverance and Transmutation in African Traditional Religions" on the persistence of African spirituality in modern Africa, Evan M. Zuesse shows that modern practices that apparently seem to deny African spirituality do in fact merely hide what he calls the "deep structure" of the African spiritual worldview that survives "intellectual rationalizations." Here again the metaphor of the burning bush and the green roots is apt. The modern African, even as a holder of three PhDs, looks at and interprets much of his or her life through African traditional spiritual windows and symbols. The question is not one of contrasting archaism and modernity of ideas; it is rather one of what idiom is useful through which to interpret and understand reality.

A critical element of the enduring past which shapes leadership perceptions and practices today is the premium placed on the "interflow of relationships," or, once again, community. A person becomes stronger as he or she integrates him or herself in a particular group or community. Of course, in African spirituality this applies union with "all things and beings," but especially with one's identifiable human community, which is an intimate composite of the living, the living-dead, the expected-living, and the community of goods, especially the land. Through this, other integrations are guaranteed. Without the assurance of belonging and its corresponding responsibilities and benefits (that is, the imperative of sharing), the status of the African leader in the community, his or her three PhDs from prestigious western universities notwithstanding, remains deeply ambivalent. He or she will be ill at ease in his or her exercise of leadership.

To understand this fact is crucially important; it will help African educationalists to design and execute curricula relevant to the present and future realities of the African continent. It will help them to take into serious account the aspect of relationships, perceived in African philosophy and religion to be central to the political and actual physical survival of the leader. The centrality of relationships or community is ignored at the cost of immense psychological dualism in the leader, ranging from local, national, and even international stages of activity.

It is unrealistic and futile to expect Africans to think in exactly the same way and act in exactly the same manner as things are done in the West, in spite of western education. If western political engagement since the Enlightenment tends to be purely secular, African political practice consists of a big dose of the mystical. It is commonly rumored that politicians of all faiths and at all levels in most countries of black Africa regularly consult diviners to guarantee or at least foretell their fortunes during elections. This does not necessarily translate into lack of political sophistication or even ruthlessness, or the total collapsing of the political and religious dimensions of life. Most of these leaders, far from being merely "naïve" and "superstitious," are in fact politically extremely shrewd, even Machiavellian. The severance of spirituality from their politics is not translated in the way that western modernism presupposes.

In Africa generally, religious belief motivates political action, where politics is understood as the art of discerning "who gets what, when and how." But this should not necessarily constitute an insurmountable obstacle to social, political and economic transformation. Although the current globalization movement carries the implicit thesis of unipolarity, there is really not one standard model of progress.

The development of democracy, economic progress, and human rights does not depend on one single model. Of course, no one today should discard democratic ideals espoused by these philosophies which, by the way, were not entirely absent from pre-modern Africa. Yet, in the same way as they were shaped and expressed differently in Europe and America, should it not be expected and possible that they should and will be shaped differently in Africa? The most appropriate question to consider is how a national entity structures its regulative, extractive, distributive, rejuvenation, and symbolic capabilities. In other words, how does a nation use its coercive power, produce and allocate goods, maintain but also adapt itself to changing circumstances, and project its values both internally and externally?

This is the present task of African leadership, something that many among the first generation of African political leaders clearly perceived and attempted to achieve. For all their mistakes, leaders like Kwame Nkrumah (Ghana), Ahmed Sekou Toure (Guinea Conakry), Leopold Sedar Senghor (Senegal), Felix Houphouet-Boigny (Cote d'Ivoire), and Kenneth Kaunda (Zambia) have bequeathed something immortal to Africa. They were aware of and articulated the need and necessity for African identity to inculturate political, economic, and social organizational ethics into the African cultural milieu. They realized that though often hidden, the African spiritual and ethical substratum is very much alive in the African psyche. In this sense inculturation is certainly not only a religious process. One exemplar contribution in this line was Julius K. Nyerere with his policy of African socialism or *Ujamaa* in Tanzania, which laid stress on the understanding of "freedom, political development, democratic decision making, welfare, and economic development" based on the African understanding of community or family-hood (*ujamaa*).

In his eleventh thesis on Feuerbach, Karl Marx pertinently pointed out that "the philosophers have only interpreted the world in various ways; the point [however] is to change it." Educationalists in Africa must not only seek to interpret the problem of leadership in Africa. They must also, and most importantly, try to see how they can change the situation. What is the approach to bring about change? What method should be used? There are two premises that should guide reflection on this issue. The process must be built on the conviction that change is desirable and that change is possible.

Change is desirable because of the debilitating dualism that we have noted that afflicts African leadership styles. They are unsure of how to act between the traditional and modern. But change is also desirable for the purpose of constructing structures that take the African environment seriously into account, leading to a truly African identity. On the practical level, change is possible. In other parts of the world, there are precedents in this line. Japan and South Korea are two countries that have managed to integrate or amalgamate their traditions and modernity amazingly successfully, so that they are strong economies, thriving democracies, and really Japanese and Korean societies in identity. This means that, although action must be taken in the present, the future is the measure of the success of the pedagogical programs to be put in place. This is implied in the above two premises about the desirability and the possibility of change.

What we need is education for critical consciousness, the capability of anyone to understand oneself in the context of his or her surrounding environment, as elaborated by Paulo Freire.[2] Paulo Freire distinguishes "critical consciousness" from "naïve consciousness" and "fanatical consciousness."

2. See Freire, *Pedagogy of the Oppressed*.

While naïve consciousness is erroneous in its perception of reality because it sees reality as static and unchangeable, and fanatical consciousness irrationally adapts itself totally to present reality in fearful or magical way, critical consciousness is "integrated with reality," subjects reality to analysis when need be, and understands reality in its proper cultural, social and historical perspective. This kind of perception usually calls for action for change.

It is easy to see how this pedagogy for critical consciousness applies to the African leadership situation. The African leader is currently debilitated by the burden of colonial inheritance which expresses itself in the pull between the two forces of tradition and modernity, community and individualism, spiritual and materialistic interpretation of life. In these circumstances, the African leader must engage in the process of self-transformation to grow toward psychological wholeness.

Chapter 14

Violence, Justice, and Reconciliation

THERE ARE FEW ISSUES today as relevant and as pressing, and more in need of some kind of solution for the sake of human and planetary survival, as the problem of destructive conflict and violence. It is also vital for theology in Africa to engage in the conversation. Theology needs to contribute ideas towards clarifying the issues involved and to suggest ways and means of realizing justice and peace in the world.

Of course, we are not faced with an entirely new issue here; reflection on conflict and violence is not novel. Questions about justice and reconciliation have been around ever since the dawn of human civilization because situations of conflict have always existed. Wars and rumors of wars, as well as accounts of cases and systems of arbitration between individuals or groups of people in conflict, or between or among nations, litter the pages of history books from very ancient times. They are the stuff of history.

Still, justification for a reflection on conflict, justice and reconciliation today arises from two facts: the fact of necessary human limitation on the one hand, but also the possibility of growth in human understanding and behavior on the other. Since time immemorial, every generation has tried to grapple with issues arising from destructive conflict, and each has arrived at some answers. Though partial, these answers have helped the people concerned to survive, hopefully with a somewhat better appreciation of what it means to live together as human beings and as creatures with other creatures on earth. Subsequent generations have built upon previous reflections to grapple with similar questions.

It is true that oftentimes what has been achieved at each point has been very little or, as some would claim, insignificant. History may not even have recorded many of these achievements. The individuals or groups of people that thought them up and tried them out may forever remain unknown and unsung. Moreover, many times the very same people may have unfortunately soon after abandoned their own contributions and reverted to previous practices of conflict and violence. This is the story that dominates history. At other times, however, we must acknowledge that the achievements have been notable. One modern example is the promulgation of the Universal Declaration of Human Rights (UDHR) by the United Nations in 1948. In asserting the universality of the rights of the human person, the document was also asserting the priority of justice in human relations.

The cynics will be quick to point out the failures of the UDHR, claiming that this particular declaration, like numerous others before and after, is often observed in the breach. If this were not the case, they argue with some justification, would we have had the various conflicts and wars that have happened after its promulgation? There is evidence now that the countries that initiated these wars did so knowingly on flimsy, fictitious grounds, frequently for the sake of their own "national interests," a euphemism for national selfishness. But the cynics need to be reminded of one thing. Because of international agreements such as the UDHR and other protocols, it has now become a little more difficult for any nation, however powerful, to initiate unwarranted aggression against another. The International Community can shame nations or groups that do so. In today's globalized world, it is very difficult for any nation to completely ignore disapproval from the International Community. The nations involved in several recent wars have not escaped international outrage and do try to save face.

Today the community of nations may have a new global situation of conflict on its hands, but on account of what others have thought and done before, it has a better perception of the consequences that conflict and violence bring about upon human beings and creation in general and therefore a better chance of avoiding them. Violence on a large scale has far more disastrous consequences in terms of destruction of human life and property than was the case, say, only a century ago. Technology has made this possible by developing incredibly efficient weapons of mass destruction (WMD) as well as vast networks of destructive mass propaganda. The kind of propaganda possible in our time brings to mind the destructive conflicts and violence being experienced in various parts of the world, resulting in a form of "clash of civilizations." In its current shape in Africa, apart from ethnic prejudices, it pits two major religious ideologies, Christianity and Islam, against each other by employing simplistic but emotionally effective labels such as "Christians are infidels" or "Muslims are terrorists." By using modern means of mass communication, crude propaganda of this kind can have as much the same devastating effect as the use of actual WMD for mass murder. This is the new situation the world is facing.

And so the moral necessity for Christians to reflect about the demands of justice and reconciliation as the antidotes against violence arises. Paul's wealth of thought on this issue is apparent above all in his hymn on Love (1 Cor 13). This hymn is the Apostle's consummate contribution to the Christian imperative of justice, reconciliation, and peace. Each generation of Christians is therefore called upon by the demands of human and Christian morality to devise social instruments and forge spiritual perceptions that cater to the imperative for human beings of reconciling with one another and with God.

To begin with, it is important to clarify some conceptual confusion that often bedevils reflection on conflict and violence. What do these notions mean? It is essential to distinguish between the ideal and the real. We have to stress the fact that practical results for justice will be obtained if these realities are handled on the practical and concrete, rather than primarily on the ideal level. Obviously, the ideal is not completely divorced from the real; it remains connected to it. The ideal is always a beacon toward ever better human performance. It acts as a constant indicator on the journey from this point to the next. The real, however, is what needs immediate attention; its examination leads to the closer attainment of the ideal. In light of this, it is necessary to make three important distinctions.

First of all, conflict is not the same thing as violence. Conflict results from the normal human struggle for individuation and identity, which are usually appreciated in a process of opposition: I am who I am because I am not the other. Individuation and identity constitute the natural process in human growth. Conflict in this case involves a situation that is certainly divisive but not inevitably violent. Recognition of this fact is the first step to reconciliation. Conflict is unavoidably present in human relationships: in this sense it is true that every person is a potential adversary. On account of the natural necessity of individuation, identity, and growth, people are different from one another. Each person has her or his own interests, recognized and acknowledged or not. For harmonious co-existence every person must constantly take account of the other person's genuine interests. Violence marks a failure in the process of mutual recognition and acceptance, regardless of whether the social entity is a family or ethnic group, or inter-religious or international one.

"Conflict resolution," therefore implies "conflict management," so that conflict does not degenerate into acts of violence. In situations of actual violence, which is a failure in resolving conflict, it is proper to talk about "violence resolution." The resolution of violence is a process that must begin with a clear understanding and appreciation of the nature of conflict. Again, conflict is not itself violence but it can be a source of violence if not properly managed. This realization is crucial for the process of violence resolution. When conflict is understood in its proper context as part of human growth, it can contribute towards preventing violence.

Another conceptual distinction pertains to the notion of justice. It is important to point out an element that is often not emphasized enough concerning justice and is in many cases even totally forgotten. While the legal and distributive dimensions of justice are essential in conflict management and violence resolution, the psychological dimension is of paramount importance in the process. Justice must not only be done, but must be seen or felt to be done. An important aspect of justice is psychological and emotional. It pertains to both the sense and the feeling of being acknowledged as a human person, and being fairly treated as a consequence.

Conflict and violence resolution do not necessarily lead to friendship. This is another distinction and clarification that must be made. In an ideal world, reconciliation would indeed mean friendship, and perhaps that is what it beckons us towards as an ultimate Christian goal. But reconciliation and friendship are distinct realities. Reconciliation can realistically be connected only with peaceful co-existence, the mutual recognition that as human beings, we all are entitled to equitable social, political and economic space in this world, seen as "communal solidarity," "social interdependence," and the "common good."

Do African indigenous perceptions on these realities have anything positive to inspire new approaches toward current situations of conflict and violence in the world?

Most states today are secular, and secular constitutions and laws direct their citizens. There is a push, even in those states that are professedly guided by religious constitutions, to distinguish between secular and religious values. Within limits, this is undoubtedly a good development, especially in a globalized multi-religious, multi-cultural world. The genuine question that religious constitutions and laws are faced with pertains to "whose religion or religious values should govern?" Considering the fact of individuation and identity discussed previously, such mono-religious, theocratic constitutions and laws tend to intensify, rather than minimize, destructive conflict between differing groups of belief systems. As a matter of fact, they easily lead to violence.

Yet, the distinction between religious and secular constitutions and processes of resolving conflict and violence should not be pushed too far. There is often a profound religious element in the human person that such processes would do well to recognize if they are to respect human rights. Indigenous African processes took this into account. In situations of potential destructive conflict and violence, African elders appealed to the authority of the ancestors as precedents, and asked them to intervene so as to heal whatever rift was threatening human and cosmic harmony. In doing so, they were recognizing the important role of the religious element in the reconciliation process. It was not for nothing in their socio-religious economy that interpersonal, inter-group, and inter-ethnic agreements and treaties were sealed by some sort of religious act, such as sacrifice and ritual meal.

The value of religious symbolism even in the life of secular states must not be underestimated. The religious dimension of the human person cannot be easily dismissed. In contemporary secular court systems, the Bible and Koran, for instance, are still important symbols of commitment to truth-telling and sincerity. Major oaths of faithfulness to service in elected leadership positions are taken using these symbols. But the question of relevance immediately arises: Do these symbols mean much to the people concerned? Do they make any difference in their attitudes and behavior? Although it is true that this is a different area of discussion, the fact that they are retained in secular states says something about the enduring religious nature of the human person that cannot be overlooked in processes of managing conflict and resolving violence. If this insight is relevant, it is important to retrieve or construct appropriate symbols that touch the hearts and minds of local communities in terms of conflict management and violence resolution. Emphasis is laid on the factor of "local situations" because it is difficult and impractical to devise grand symbols that would speak to all peoples in all situations. Such symbols end up being irrelevant, speaking to people only superficially, if at all. As a rule, they are unable to bring about the communal solidarity, social interdependence, and the common good that bring about justice.

In the best of circumstances, symbols that speak meaningfully to everyone regardless of cultural and other differences would be preferable. However, the truth is that this is not possible. Different symbols and rituals are necessary for different people. If, for example, a certain sacrifice, say in the Turkana religious world, marks and mandates cessation of hostilities for the Turkana, it would be the equivalent of a treaty or a pact under oath, marking and mandating the same thing in another society, say the British. Thus, even though the full significance and implications of the sacrifice on the one hand, and the oath on the other, would be fully understood only in each of the respective communities, the goal of the resolution of destructive conflict and violence would nevertheless be served between them, for it would be the sincere intention of each of the actions, speaking deeply only to each of the parties but tending to the same goal for both. The trans-cultural element here would be the intention and the goal, not necessarily the ritual act *per se*.

The deeper meaning of justice shapes social relationships through mutual recognition and respect. The principle of recognition and respect determines the whole process. There can be no attempt at meaningful justice where parties in conflict refuse to accept and respect the rightful existence of each other, the *humanum* of the other. In this matter, factual existence as a human person is of secondary importance to the process of justice; it is rather the psychological, mental, and emotional acceptance of it in the other that deserves the emphasis. If this "right of existence" is not recognized, accepted, and respected, the psychological and often concrete practical tendency is usually to try to wipe out the other, or at least that part of the other the other deems offensive. And because this feeling of denigration in conflict and violence is often mutual, it becomes difficult to break the spread and spiral of violence. Violence and its accompanying language of defeat or surrender, submission or occupation, and so on, reflect this psychological reality.

Recognition and respect of the other's existence implies the necessity of accommodation: concretely the concession that we are all entitled to this geographical, social, political, economic or whatever spaces that we happen to share. That we are all here, sharing this space, may be an accident for some, or, for Christian believers, a result of divine design. But in either case, it is a given, regardless of whether or not we like it. Destructive conflict and violence arise out of the fact that people fail to negotiate successfully enough who will occupy which slice of the available space. In other words, there is failure in justice when there is lack of recognition of the personal of corporate individuality and identity of the other or others and their place in the world. Inevitably it is a failure that leads to violence.

The general African cultural validation of the person as person, entitled to shelter, food, and drink, regardless of place of origin, should help correct the tendency to bias in this sphere. This is best illustrated in traditional practices of land division and ownership, or the use of water resources, where strangers were accommodated even though they were not yet completely integrated into the clan or ethnic group. Underlying the practice was the appreciation that land, water and so on are the essence of life, and so they cannot be separated from life force. From the perspective of indigenous African ethics, to withhold any of them from a person would be a grave form of injustice. To many ears today, this claim might seem ridiculously exaggerated presented as an African contribution to violence resolution, what with the bloody events in Rwanda, Burundi, the Democratic Republic of Congo (DRC), South Africa, and so on, as a consequence of the reluctance to share some of these things. However, without wishing to deny that there were loopholes in the traditional practical procedures of distribution of life's resources, it is also important not to overlook the intrusion and corruption of these arrangements in Africa by very aggressive foreign perceptions and practices that have taken place over a period of two centuries and more.

The inspiration in traditional visions of justice rests more clearly in the moral acceptance of responsibility for the life of the other in its basic needs for survival. Yet, on account of national boundaries and the associated social, political, economic, ideological, and religious concerns, recognition of this moral responsibility is greatly limited in contemporary experience. Most often, it is ignored or denied.

The purpose and goal of resolving destructive conflict and violence is finding solutions in the form of reconciliation through dialogue or sincere communication. In contemporary political and economic arrangements, the process may be referred to as negotiation. Unfortunately, much of what is today called "negotiation" in international, intra-national, inter-group, or interpersonal destructive conflict and violence rests in the category of manipulation rather than real communication. But if resolution of destructive conflict and violence is to come about, it will be due to the degree that genuine communication happens. If any agreement achieved unravels, it is also to the extent that dialogue as communication of meaning breaks up.

The Church may often not have a big part to play in the actual dynamics of resolution of destructive conflict and violence, but it has a fundamental role in building its spirit. It is a process that must begin and be maintained in the very life-fabric of the Church itself. The Church must be ready to listen and talk to others in inter-religious and ecumenical dialogue, demonstrating by its own life the fact that tolerance and coexistence are possible. When religions and faiths do this through their visible structures, they contribute to the processes of reconciliation and peacemaking by addressing issues in the same spirit of tolerance they already carry from within. The realization that politics and religion are both at the service of life is fundamental to both. The deepest meaning and requirement of religion and politics consists in their convergence in essentials, not in flight from each another. Convergence becomes an instrument of reconciliation, justice and peace.

It is not possible to understand the power of dialogue as an instrument of reconciliation from the African perspective without appreciating the role that the word plays in the African palaver or popular council. In black Africa, particularly in a palaver situation, the word can be said to have a life-or-death power. The word that addresses justice, peace, and reconciliation means primarily uttered speech, but it goes beyond it. As a reflection of one's entire being and personality the word implies certain attitudes or body language, in the form of a glance, for example, or the entire personal demeanor projected in the process of the palaver. These possess the power to heal or kill. The word is the manifestation of the Spirit, of the whole being or person. So it matters very much how the word is used. Let everyone speak in a palaver, but let them speak with due reverence to the word of the other. If it is to heal, the reconciling goal of the palaver, despite the complexity that the process always involves, must be clear to all. The palaver is intended as an instrument for casting away the evil of violence, which destroys the power of life. But it is intended as an instrument for bringing about reconciliation because it builds up the vitality of humanity and creation.

Although as part of human fallibility violence cannot be completely eliminated from human life, Christian faith leads to the hope that it can and will be overcome. One meaning of the resurrection of Jesus Christ lies in this theological conviction, that Jesus suffered violence in order to defeat it, to rise above it, to liberate or "redeem" human beings from it. Violence may be part of fallen human existence, but reconciliation is part of liberated human life. This was certainly Paul's hope when he declared that the time would come when God will be the consummation of everything (see Rom 8:22-23). But this was not only an eschatological hope for Paul. The time for reconciling ourselves with God must start here and now. It is imperative that humanity must work out its salvation now "with fear and trembling" (Phil 2:12). The strategy is to submit to God by reining in the evil desires that are a result of human pride and greed (see Jas 4:13-17).

"Blessed are the peacemakers," Jesus taught (Matt 5:9). The peacemakers are the children of God because they are doing what God wants, which is struggling for justice and peace. Those who struggle for peace and reconciliation are God's ambassadors. They recall the image of peaceful innocence and coexistence painted by Isaiah the prophet. Humanity lost it but Jesus came to re-establish it (see Isa 11:5-9). The peace of Jesus is something the world must struggle for. Nations must learn to "beat their swords into plowshares and their spears into pruning hooks. One nation shall not raise the sword against another, nor shall they train for war again" (Isa 2:4).

Chapter 15

Human Sexuality in Africa

IN THE INTERACTION THAT is taking place between tradition and modernity in Africa, the question of human sexuality forms part of the discussion. From the fairly stable life of the village and single ethnic community regulated by well-known customs, attitudes, and sexual mores in the past, life today, especially in towns and cities, does not respect such guarantees, especially for the youth. The existing interface of opinions and practices is often disorienting, even chaotic for some. Many people in Africa do not know where to stand in issues of sexual morality and ethics.

The behavior of adults and the youth oftentimes portrays different or contradictory expectations. The mass media, now spread to the remotest villages of the continent, does not promote a consistent sexual ethic either. Whereas the Churches uphold a conservative message toward sexuality and sexual relations, the media is by and large rather permissive, generally selling the moral that sexual activity is all right as long as nobody gets hurt.

Given this situation, questions that used to have straightforward answers in indigenous societies are now very complex and difficult to address. What is marriage? Is polygamy as practiced in many African traditions still acceptable? What about the dignity of the woman and the girl-child, especially in situations of rape or early marriages? How about prostitution: should it continue to be criminalized or should it be legalized, as some are demanding? Is the question of abortion relevant only in relation to a woman's "right to her own body?" Should abortion be criminalized as murder, the killing of innocent life or should it be left to the discretion of individual consciences depending on circumstances, such as in cases of rape, incest, or to protect the life of the mother? Can abortion practices be harmonized with the "blessing" of many children in indigenous spirituality? What is sex education? Is it important to the youth in a situation of HIV and AIDS? How should it be offered, and by whom?

The list of issues is almost endless. Today questions are being raised concerning what to do about polygamy, rites of passage such as female circumcision, bride wealth, and widow inheritance. In the Church, divorce and remarriage, trial marriages, single-family homes, and homosexuality are vexing. There are also issues of pornography and pre-marital intercourse. The question these modern issues prompt is whether there can be African responses to them, taking into account the African social spiritual context of the supremacy of the value of life and its preservation. But it is precisely at this point where complex questions have become even more so. What is the meaning of "life" and, in the expended understanding, what are the methods to promote it? Is this restricted to the use of physical generative aspects alone in sexual relations, or does it imply much more than this? Are not the elements of love and peace also necessary dimensions of the flourishing of life? It is only possible to briefly discuss here a few examples of African social and theological imagination vis-à-vis situations raised by modernity.

Let us begin with the institution of marriage. In the last sixty years or so, there have been many changes that have impacted the institution of marriage in Africa. An area that is being hotly debated is plural marriage, or marriage between one man and several women. It was taken for granted in indigenous African culture and is still practiced today, and not only in rural areas. President Jacob Zuma of South Africa, for instance, has several wives and justifies it on the basis of Zulu (African) culture. Another extreme and rare case is that of King Mswati III of Swaziland who is allowed to pick a virgin wife every year. Christianity in many of its mainline denominations is, however, against this practice on moral grounds. In the contemporary African context where there is such a broad range of disparate opinions, none of which can claim absolute moral certainty, can there be any compromise between them? How can they be approached in Africa?

Polygamy and its associated practices of levirate and wife inheritance unions must be approached within the context of human dignity and rights, especially of the woman. In this regard, more than any other approach, some African governments have taken a wiser, more ethical path. They have enacted three categories of marriage to which the prospective couple must assent: by law, marriage must be monogamous, polygamous, or potentially polygamous, and the prospective wife or husband has the legal right to opt for any one form among these. It seems that this approach is the one that best respects the conscience and dignity of both partners as well as their religious and cultural sensibilities and freedom. Christians, of course, would contract the sacrament of matrimony according to the monogamous standard, but they would respect the other forms as true marriages, for although Christian teaching nurtured in the West categorically condemns the practice of polygamy, the Scriptures seem to be silent about it.

Again, from the point of view of the rather restricted physicalist perception of the promotion of life, the general attitude towards homosexuality and homosexual relations in Africa has been one of denial or disavowal. From the religious and aesthetic point of view, homosexuality is threatening to indigenous African societies because it does not promote physical life. Thus, it is repressed psychologically in the individual, and in society in general it is often accompanied by strong censure. Does this mean, however, that people with the homosexual orientation did not exist in Africa, as it is sometimes dishonestly claimed? Despite suggestions that it is a result of influence from "the West," the fact that more and more African men and women are coming out to publicly own their gay and lesbian sexuality is disproving the denial.

Do gay- or lesbian-oriented people have the right to express this orientation in loving, permanent relationships and unions such as heterosexuals do? By and large, the jury is still out on this, but it would seem that respect for human rights and dignity demand that society and the Church acknowledge this. The recent and ongoing worldwide controversy over homosexuality in the Anglican Communion has been over how Scripture is interpreted on this question. There are some who argue that the Bible categorically rejects it in any form and damns anyone with either the orientation or indulging in homosexual activity because, according to their perception, "it is against nature" (see Gen 19:4–11, Lev 18:22, Rom 1:24–32, 1 Cor 6:9, and 1 Tim 1:10). But there are those who urge tolerance, arguing that what little the Bible has to say about it, like so many other things, reflects social understanding of the time which does not warrant such uncompromising verdict today. From a Christian faith perspective, the counsel about the centrality of love in all relationships makes sense even on this question and cannot be dismissed offhand.

Because of the disruption of the indigenous African family by modernity, young adults do not have the benefit of the presence of grandfathers or grandmothers, uncles or aunts, to instruct them from early on about the basic "facts of life" as it used to be in the past. But even today, apart from the fact that there is disagreement whether or not "sex education" should be provided in schools, there is no consensus about what it constitutes. Some interpret it as provision of knowledge about prophylactics and birth control methods. Since they are going to engage in sexual activity anyway, seems to be the logic of this, they had better be taught how to do it without health risks to themselves and their partners. Others, however, maintain that sex education consists in instilling in young people the necessity to abstain from genital sexual relations until marriage. This is the position of most Christian Churches. But perhaps the issue today should involve a search for contemporary alternative rites of passage in the Church and society at large to replace those that were eliminated by Christianity and modern education.

There is no question that some indigenous rites of passage are clearly distasteful and, as part of instituting new ones, should be stopped. But there is no need to make people who practice certain customs in good faith look cruel or stupid, even if, clearly, such customs should be eliminated. The issue is one of correcting a wrong, not of casting aspersions on entire communities. The task in initiation rites is to distinguish which among the practices served as positive and to educate people to reject the negative.

A social aspect of sexuality that still confronts many communities in Africa concerns the stigmatization of people who are HIV-positive. How are these people treated in government and in the Churches? Are they discriminated against in employment, in insurance policies, in joining recreational facilities? What is the teaching of the Churches about the pandemic and HIV-positive people? Are they discreetly labeled as sinners, unworthy of the mercy of God? One element that governments should try to address on the issue of HIV and AIDS relates to economics. The whole story of HIV and AIDS cannot be told without reference to poverty, powerlessness, and marginalization of women in society. Although he was disparaged then, Thabo Mbeki, at that time president of South Africa, was right to make this link in a speech in 2000.

Sexual activity with minors is another problem connected with sexuality. The behavior is abhorrent and it becomes much more repulsive when it involves an adult, such as a teacher or a priest, who is entrusted with care for the young to whom, in their innocence, children usually give their total trust. Popular horror is perfectly justified in such cases. The victims' testimonies testify to that anguish, and psychological studies now confirm that the pain and wounds inflicted on children by such immoral and shameful deeds during the most innocent and vulnerable period of their lives cannot be completely healed.

It is necessary to acknowledge that child sexual abuse cannot be relegated to only western societies. It affects African societies and the Church there as well. At any one time and place some people in the population are sexually attracted to minors. As elsewhere, sexual molestation of minors happens in Africa in families, neighborhoods, schools, Churches, and so on. The media here also sometimes carry stories of brutal sexual abuses against children, and even infants. In South Africa, for example, we hear of the foolish belief among some people there that having sex with virgins, usually children, is a cure for AIDS! So whatever differences exist in this matter between Africa and the West, they are generally of degree, not of actuality. The sooner this is realized in Africa, the better. Then, instead of continuing to pretend that what happens does not, society would be better prepared to take the necessary steps to combat the hazard. "If you watch your pot, your food will not burn."

In the Catholic Church in Africa, suspicion is usually directed to celibate clergy and religious because society generally views lifelong celibacy or virginity negatively. So, it merely serves to confirm an already strongly established bias when a member of the clergy or religious happens to be implicated in pedophile acts. Still, despite the myth that celibacy is the source of pedophilia, the Church needs to take a long look at its teaching about human sexuality, especially as it pertains to the clergy. It must update her perception of and position, as new and more accurate understandings on human biology, psychology, sociology and spirituality emerge concerning this fundamental fact of human life. If the Church must always be reformed, surely one of the areas which should be looked into today is its teaching on human sexuality.

Whereas celibacy as a gift or *charism* from God is not in question, its interpretation as rejection of sexuality as constitutive of the human person is inaccurate. More so, the understanding of celibacy as a rejection of sensuality, tenderness and mutuality must be re-examined. This negative and unhealthy perception of the charism of celibacy and virginity as a state of being sexless and unfeeling has survived for far too long in Catholic Christianity and has often caused a lot of harm to certain members of the clergy by stunting their human growth. It is essentially a Manichaean view, suggesting contempt or, worse, fear of the body. As such, it is manifestly un-African and unchristian. According to St. Gregory of Nyssa, what Christ did not assume, he did not heal (*"Quod [Christus] non assumpsit, non sanavit"*). If Christ assumed a human body, he healed the body. We might even quote the divine message to the still bigoted Peter: "what God has made clean, you are not to call profane" (Acts 10:15).

The Catholic faithful have, of course, the right to expect a high degree of ethical standards in the behavior of their leaders. After all, the institution of the priesthood claims for itself a certain moral authority. Thus society as a whole is justified in being more demanding of the priest in moral rectitude than of any other of its members. The critical pastoral question for bishops is what to do with clerics under their charge who abuse both their vocation and popular trust by sexually molesting minors. As shepherds of both the abused and the abuser, this is not an easy question. The recent debate in the West on the issue rightly lays emphasis on the protection of the innocence of children as a priority. It urges that the offending priest should immediately be defrocked, reported to the civil authorities and, if convicted, be made to pay for his crime. While one can see and appreciate the point of this argument, one must also say that it fails to fully take into account the love of Christ for sinners. Can justice be balanced with compassion and vice versa? Without justice, the process of healing for the victims cannot begin, but without compassion justice is vindictive. Inspired by African culture, where the integrity of community is imperative, perhaps the Church in Africa can attempt other approaches towards dealing with the issue, a combination of justice and compassion.

From the African communitarian perspective, pedophilia as a crime touches one of the most central elements of the community. In hurting vulnerable children, it puts the future existence of the community in jeopardy. This should be clear in the context of the Church. How can the Church remain a healthy community of love if its most vulnerable members are hurt from within? It is essential, therefore, that those responsible for recruitment to the priesthood must try to detect the problem of pedophilia in those applying to prepare for the priesthood. Sciences such as psychology should be of help here.

For those already in the priesthood, a process of purification must take place, and this, will happen only when a "Council of Elders" in the form of the Parish Council or a "Circle of Sages" is empowered to play its proper autonomous role in the parish, school, orphanage, and so on, not as an appendage of clerical authority, but as guardians of the Christian community. Present structures where decisions in this matter must come from the bishop, cannot address this issue quickly enough or adequately enough when it arises. People who are in a position to actually know their priest are the parishioners or the priest's immediate coworkers. Can they, through their Parish Council or Circle of Sages, advise, reprimand, and even censure an offending priest? This now seems to be imperative.

Although the Church has up to now not dared to put this structurally into practice, many official documents of the Church since Vatican II have consistently reiterated it. The "Final Message" of the second special assembly for Africa of the Synod of Bishops of 2009 (no. 22), affirms the role of the laity in these words:

> This Synod turns with deep affection to the lay faithful of Africa. You are the Church of God in the market place of society. It is in and through you that the life and witness of the Church are made visible to the world. You therefore share the mandate of the Church to be "ambassadors for Christ" working for reconciliation

of people to God and among themselves. This requires of you to allow your Christian faith to permeate every aspect and facet of your lives; in the family, at work, in the professions, in politics and public life.[1]

What control mechanism will there be for these Councils or Circles? No one should dismiss some problems the structural empowerment of the laity may cause, including false accusations against innocent priests, divisions in the parish for and against a particular priest, and so on. Yet, this approach has the benefit of transparency and accountability to the people immediately affected by the priest's behavior. It is no foolproof solution, but there is also something to be said in favor of communities hiring and firing their pastors because it encourages integrity and accountability among the pastors to those they serve.

---

1. Message to the People of God, "Assembly for Africa of the Synod of Bishops," n. 22

Chapter 16

An African Reading of "Charity in Truth"

Pope Benedict XVI's Encyclical letter *Caritas in Veritate* ("Charity in Truth") was published on 29 June 2009. It is a significant addition to the body of literature called the Social Teaching of the Church (STC) that insists that faith is empty without the practice of justice. According to the STC, social concern is not something apart from the Gospel but is an indispensable tool to foster the divine plan for salvation, the construction of God's kingdom on earth.

In the letter, Pope Benedict XVI develops in particular the thought of his two most immediate predecessors, Pope Paul VI (1963–78) and Pope John Paul II (1978–2005). The writings of both of these Popes contributed significantly to the theological understanding of justice, human rights and dignity and international relations in the political, economic, and social context of the latter half of the twentieth century. In *Caritas in Veritate*, Pope Benedict XVI wants to apply their insight to the current global environment.

Situating this Encyclical letter of Pope Benedict XVI in the context of the African continent, and for reasons that will presently become clear, it is possible to re-christen it as "Truth is Charity." This is not to downplay the force of the letter's original title, which is argued quite eloquently by the Pope himself. Yet, seen from the context of the history and overall present situation of Africa, to speak about truth as charity possesses a two-fold advantage. On the one hand, it is more evocative of where the African people have been, and, on the other, it is more indicative of where they need to go in terms of charity and truth.

It is easy to appreciate that the history of the African continent and its peoples in general is pervaded by a high degree of conceptual inaccuracies and outright falsehoods, particularly its history of development. It is true that some people are annoyed about hearing this again and again and would rather we quit "the blame game," as they see it, and get on with the business of real change and development. Nevertheless, it is essential for people to remember their history, not primarily for the sake of blame, but in order to learn from its lessons. The path to integral development in Africa may lie in understanding the past. It is important for authentic development to comprehend the sources of the untruth about Africa and its peoples. These falsehoods are born of stereotyping and generalizations about Africa from outside. Whether Africans themselves have internalized and regurgitate them in development rhetoric makes little difference to the reality of the nature of the distortions.

What, for example, is "undeveloped" or "underdeveloped" about Africa? These words are now rarely used as such, but the attitudes they represent are still very much alive in the perceptions of the continent both from within and from outside of it. In modern terms, what is underdevelopment, and on what criteria is the underdevelopment of Africa premised? And what constitutes the real development of the continent? Is it material wealth in an environment of psychological or political bondage? Could it really be a high gross national product percentage number along with actual poverty of a substantial section of the national population? Does development mean the availability of only material infrastructures that serve the elite at the expense of the majority of people in a nation? Isn't the cultural identity and dignity of the people also an indispensable indicator of authentic development?

Between the mid-1960s and the mid-1980s, the United Nations launched two phases of development decades. At the beginning of 1988, it inaugurated a third decade of development, this time dedicated to culture. Assessing the performance of the previous two decades, the United Nations Educational, Scientific and Cultural Organization (UNESCO) admitted that its shortcoming consisted in emphasizing material progress at the expense of cultural development. Both UNESCO and the Secretary General of the UN admitted that the previous attempts had failed to reach some of their goals because not enough attention had been paid to culture. As UNESCO put it:

> A review of the first two international development decades has shown that the concept of development based solely on quantitative material growth leads to dead-ends. The review substantiates the principle that cultural factors must be taken into consideration

in any innovative undertaking, and that cultural development is not only a qualitative corrective to economic and social development but also the ultimate purpose of progress.[1]

It is important for African populations to appreciate this so as to forge for themselves the kind of progress proper to them, in which cultural values serve both as a starting point and criteria of development's progress. This is why it is necessary to be truthful about African history and about the continent's present political, economic, and social realities. This is why, in this context, truth is charity.

In his letter, Pope Benedict XVI attempts to expose truth about the situation of the world today using the tradition of the social thought of the Church, and in so doing he is being charitable. As he himself explains, charity may be the goal, but the foundation of development is truth because "truth preserves and expresses charity's power to liberate in the ever-changing events of history." True development needs truth, he affirms. "Without truth, without trust and love for what is true," the Pope argues, "there is no social conscience and responsibility, and social action ends up serving private interests and the logic of power, resulting in social fragmentation, especially in a globalized society at difficult times like the present" (no. 5). Without truth, social action may end up being oppressive and exploitative.

Authentic development in Africa must depend first and above all upon the successful deconstruction of the falsehoods about the African continent and the African person. Concretely in Africa, the historical experiences of slavery and colonialism, both of which have fundamentally influenced the shape of development in the continent, were based on one, single, defining falsehood: the inferiority of the enslaved or colonized African at one notional end. At the other end as corollary to it, there was the perceived superiority of the slave owner or colonizing societies. At both ends, the falsehood developed into a culture and dictated the understanding and shape of development.

The truth about the African person as a human person and African societies as possessing of their own civilizations brought about the social and psychological emancipation of the African person from the chains of slavery and the indignity of colonialism. Again, as corollary, it served to set afoot the process of psycho-socially freeing the slaver and colonialist from the mental and attitudinal slavery of racial prejudice. These processes are admittedly not yet complete, but without the initial struggle for truth they may well have not even begun.

1. World Decade for Cultural Development, "World Decade for Cultural Development, 1988-1997: plan of action," accessed April 24, 2016. http://www.unesdoc/unesco.org/images/0008/000852/085291eb.pdf.

In attempting to spell out the truth about human society vis-à-vis the political, economic and social order universally, Pope Benedict XVI is at the same time being at the service of this task in Africa. Charity in truth, yes, but only the absolute truth about the function of economics and politics locally and internationally in this age of globalization can be capable of serving charity. "The truth of globalization as a process and its fundamental ethical criterion are given by the unity of the human family and its development towards what is good" (no. 42). It is only by being honest and truthful about world order that is based on the "commitment . . . *to promote a person-based and community-oriented cultural process of world-wide integration that is open to transcendence*" can we begin the process of bringing about just relationships among people and nations (no. 42). Only then can we begin the process of liberating social structures around the world in favor of promoting integral development and authentic freedom. This is the function of truth for charity. Ultimately, this is true charity.

For Pope Benedict XVI, development has universal ethical dimensions. The Pope insists, nevertheless, that we must understand the ethics of development in its proper sense as a process "which is people-oriented," intended to achieve "human and social ends" on the basis of the recognition of the "inviolable dignity of the human person and the transcendent value of natural moral norms" (nos. 45–46). Thus, "in *development programs*, the principle of the *centrality of the human person*, as the subject primarily responsible for development, must be preserved." According to the Pope, "the principal [ethical] concern must be to improve the actual living conditions of the people in a given region, thus enabling them to carry out those duties which their poverty does not presently allow them to fulfill" (no. 47).

Whereas in former times this was possible to do in limited geographical and social spheres, this is not the case today. Today, development on both the sociological and theological level is a global issue on account of the reality of universal human interconnectedness. "In an increasingly globalized society, the common good and the effort to obtain it cannot fail to assume the dimensions of the whole human family," the Pope writes. This means, concretely, the engagement of "the community of peoples and nations, in such a way as to shape the *earthly city* in unity and peace, rendering it to some degree an anticipation of the undivided *city of God*." This is inescapable "in a world that is becoming progressively and pervasively globalized." According to the Pope, "the risk of our time is that the de facto interdependence of people and nations is not matched by ethical interaction of consciences and minds that would give rise to truly human development" (nos. 7–9).

Following Pope Paul VI, Pope Benedict XVI therefore looks at the truth of development in terms of the interaction on both the material and psycho-social or spiritual levels of individual persons and the human community, the growth of "every person and of all humanity." Integrity or wholeness is a key notion here: the quality of the integrity of the individual person and that of the community of persons (the human race) in relation to itself and to one another is what is at stake. What is it that makes a person integral or whole in relation to him- or herself and to the human community on the one hand, and what makes the society integral or whole in relation to itself and the individual within it on the other? These are the questions for true development. They go beyond the material consequences of human relationships and have to do also, and perhaps primarily, with spiritual values. Fundamental to these values, as Pope Benedict XVI sees things, is freedom.

Emphasizing the centrality of truth as charity, the Pope understands that truth is the condition for freedom. He has in mind here the words of Jesus in John 8:32: "... you will know the truth, and the truth will set you free." For Pope Benedict XVI, freedom is in turn a condition for true charity. "Fidelity to man requires *fidelity to the truth*, which alone is the *guarantee of freedom*" (no. 9). Untruth is slavery in a real sense. All discrimination, oppression, and murder between and among human beings are founded above all on certain untruths or false conceptual constructs about persons and communities. These may take the form of cultural, philosophical, anthropological, or theological biases.

Freedom founded on truth is the only kind of freedom that facilitates true charity or love; and this is the kind of love that alone makes people true children of God. The passage in the Gospel according to John makes it clear: "If you remain in my word, you will truly be my disciples, and you will know the truth, and the truth will set you free" (John 8:31). But it is not enough to know the truth. To be faithful to the complete dynamics of truth, one must also tell the truth: "I tell you what I have seen in the Father's presence." Further, truth cannot remain theoretical; it must be completed by action in the form of ethical behavior. Without ethical behavior life is a lie. As Jesus urges the Jews: "do what you have heard from the Father" (John 8:38).

Ethical behavior is for Jesus crucial to truth. This justifies the title of Pope Benedict XVI's letter, "Charity in Truth." In John's Gospel, Jesus insists on the point, emphasizing that ethical behavior is what makes one a child of God. Whoever claims to be of God must live and act in the manner God wants. According to John, Jesus' adversaries are on the wrong side of truth because, although they claim to be children of Abraham, a good and just man, they lack charity. They hate Jesus and want to do him harm. But only the evil one, "who was a murderer from the beginning and does not stand in truth, because there is no truth in him," would do such thing. Knowing and doing the truth is the supreme form of love. In the social sphere, truth involves avoiding the fundamental lie about the inequality of human beings. This is the source of every kind of oppression and murder.

As well, Pope Benedict XVI finds inspiration for his letter from Paul's letter to Corinthians. From there, he develops the idea that "to defend the truth, to articulate it with humility and conviction, and to bear witness to it in life are . . . exacting and indispensable forms of charity" (no. 1). What the Pope exposes is that three interconnected dimensions comprise the manifestation of charity: the epistemological dimension of knowing the truth, the demonstrative dimension of speaking the truth, and the practical dimension of living the truth in love. The first two involve orthodoxy, the latter orthopraxis. All are equally important.

The Pope appeals to the Catholic faithful to enter into the process of knowing, telling and practicing the truth in the context of the contemporary socio-economic environment of peoples and nations. Attentiveness to this Christian calling leads to a life of charity that "gives real substance to the personal relationship with God and with neighbor" on both the small- and large-scale dimensions of human existence (no. 2). Underlying Pope Benedict XVI's thought in this letter is once again the conviction that truth inspired by God in social, political, and economic matters is the best expression of charity.

There are three major myths among others that must be psychologically and practically refuted and expunged from general perceptions of the African continent so as to put the process of African development on an authentic path. They involve distorted claims about the material, moral, and intellectual resources of Africa. The falsity of the allegations that Africa lacks these resources for its own development must be exposed.

The first element of the allegations is the most easily debunked. If Africa attracts the attention of the world today, as in the past, it is mainly also because of her abundant material resources. Paradoxically, many of the current woes of the continent can be attributed to this fact. It is not for lack of material resources that Africans do not "do more, know more and have more in order to be more" and so also contribute to the universal human common good as subjects. This situation is not "due to chance or historical necessity," as Pope Benedict XVI correctly points out. In Africa, it is "attributable to human responsibility" in the form of the historical and current practices of exploitation of the continent (no. 17–18).

The further claim that Africa lacks the moral resources for development touches the spiritual aspect of the African worldview. Western Christianity has historically demonized African religiosity on this account. Considering the fact that the Christianization of Africa was understood to be at the same time a process of civilization, the spiritual values of African Religion concerning the essential community of persons and goods were dismissed out of hand. For this reason, Africa's contribution in understanding and proper handling of capital, labor relations, production, and so on, was ignored. Yet as Pope Benedict XVI warns, "*business management cannot concern itself only with the interests of the proprietors, but must also assume responsibility for all other stakeholders who contribute to the life of business.*" These include "the workers, the clients, the suppliers of various elements of production, the community of reference" (no. 40). The communitarian aspect of African spirituality of the living, living-dead, yet-to-be-born and social goods might have inspired serious attention to this requirement. The African spiritual worldview of the interconnectedness of all creation in the interest of life, or what Pope Benedict XVI describes as the "*covenant between human beings and the environment*" (no. 50)—might also have inspired respect for the environment which is being destroyed by human economic activity, almost without regard for future generations. Like the Pope, African spirituality regards creation as a gift from God "which we may use responsibly to satisfy our legitimate needs, material or otherwise, while respecting the intrinsic balance of creation" (no. 48–50).

Human responsibility is also involved with regard to the intellectual dimension of the development of Africa, and here education is the issue. Ever since it was introduced in the continent, the western education system has emphasized the aspect of imitation rather than innovation as the basic value of educational training. In this way, it has stultified the development of the African imagination in proposing solutions relevant to the specific environment of the continent. This is evident in the political and economic organization in place in Africa, despite a rich history of alternative political and economic systems to be found there. Uncritical imitation can also be seen in the cultural and social spheres where, on account of the influence of the media of mass communication, western values are indiscriminately imported into the continent. No one is suggesting cultural insularity, which apart from being undesirable and ultimately impoverishing, is impossible today. What is needed, as an element of development, is a firm cultural identity. This must be taken as a criterion of the principle of cultural sharing or cross-fertilization. In political, economic and cultural activity, Africans must not lose their role as "creators," and cultural identity can enable them to be so.

Globalization's impelling force and goal is to homogenize the world in almost every respect, and no nation can escape the grasp of this movement. For better or worse, its impact straddles the most remote corners of the world. The only question it presents is not whether to accept it, to which there seems to be no choice. The challenge for both micro and macro societies such as nations is how to manage it. Globalization, Pope Benedict XVI says, must not be "viewed in fatalistic terms, as if the dynamics involved were the product of anonymous impersonal forces or structures independent of the human will." On the contrary, it is a consequence of human will and agency. "The truth of globalization as a process and its fundamental ethical criterion are given by the unity of the human family and its development towards what is good" (no. 42).

During the Second African Synod, the African bishops recognized the inevitability of the globalization movement and spoke of how it affects Africa, given the continent's situation of political and economic instability. Like the Pope, the bishops pointed out in Proposition 31 that as a movement, globalization is not value-free, especially in its consequences; it contains "ambiguities" for the people of Africa, they said. It is these ambiguities that the Church in Africa must vigorously counteract because, as custodian of the Good News of Jesus Christ, it has an inescapable obligation in this sphere. The Church has to "be ready to respond to the challenges that globalization entails and confront them responsibly."[2]

Globalization's ambiguities and challenges consist in its key tendency to benefit only a section of the world's population, notably the already materially affluent, and so to deny or withdraw any kind of self-exercising power from the poor over themselves as people and over their resources. Some benefits for the poor may accrue from the movement, but generally not in the economic spheres. As it is now, globalization's overall effect for the poor is intensifying disempowerment and deepening material and cultural impoverishment. For both the bishops and the Pope, this is what must not be tolerated. The immediate challenge, then, is what to do? What action, flowing from the word of God, may be envisaged?

The African bishops' general response is pertinent to the points Pope Benedict XVI makes. The bishops' point is that "the best globalization must be a globalization of solidarity" (Proposition no. 31). By solidarity, they mean the purpose of transformation of lives from a less to a more human level. This requires the community of nations struggling to uphold justice, peace, and harmony universally.

The theology of solidarity proceeds from God's fundamental solidarity with the human race and with all of creation. Considering God is Creator this is not surprising, and the Hebrew Scriptures testify to the fact by insisting

---

2. "La Santa Sede," Synodus Episcoporum: Ii Coetus Specialis Pro Africa, accessed June 18, 2016. http://portal.unesco.org/culture/en/files/12762/11295421661mexico_en.pdf/mexico_en.pdf

from the very beginning that God saw creation as "good." This is further confirmed by the history of Israel, which is theologically indicative of all human history on earth, where God's care and concern for the people is unquestionable, in spite, and even because of, the latter's frequent lapses of accountability. In advocating the establishment and maintenance of divine order on earth, the Hebrew prophets were advocating the process of transformation of society. They were thus in solidarity with all of those suffering from the negative consequences of unjust structures and behavior.

The life of Jesus, as interpreted by the Evangelists and all the other authors whose works form the canon of the New Testament, has as its basic notion, the transforming struggle in solidarity with humans. Technically, this is described as the call to *metanoia* or repentance, a change of heart in favor of human and human-divine communion. The early Christian writers, when they talked about wealth and the imperative of equitable distribution of the fruits of the earth, had solidarity both as their point of departure and goal. Because Jesus' life and teaching derives its meaning from God's solidarity with humanity or, in other words, God's plan for human liberation and fulfillment, solidarity becomes an imperative for integral development. It is for this reason that solidarity is binding for all Christian believers. It constitutes a moral law, even if it is also founded on natural reason.

It is important to emphasize on this point the element of African communitarianism. Authentic humanity or integral human development was measured by this criterion, not only in terms of material wealth. Development was gauged in terms of the role that wealth played as an instrument of social cohesion. The basic question was not how much wealth or other endowments distinguished a person from others, but how much it integrated the individual within society in terms of their spirit of generosity and sharing for the sake of their own wellbeing and that of their family, clan and tribe.

In this regard, Pope Benedict XVI makes a most striking assertion. He affirms that "one of the deepest forms of poverty a person can experience is isolation" (no. 53). African ethics understood the meaning of this in terms of the importance it placed on belonging to and participating in family and clan and the reciprocity it implied and called for by this requirement. With the rise of individualistic ethics, not enough attention is placed today on the aspect of belonging in development discourse, and this is what Pope Benedict XVI warns the world to correct. The depth of communion between and among individuals and nations, not the degree of difference or isolation from others, is the ethical ideal and demand. As in traditional African ethics, it ought to be the criterion for the good life (i.e., development) of the individual and society. For Africa to anchor the future of its development on its cultural past, this is the sort of thing that must be taken into account because it is what true solidarity in a globalized world means.

From the point of view of authentic human development, practical solidarity should mean more than mere co-operation or collaboration between and among nations. It demands, rather, and first of all, the deeper realization and conviction that "*the human race is a single family* working together in true communion, not simply a group of subjects who happen to live side by side." "The theme of development can be identified with the inclusion-in-relation of all individuals and peoples within the one community of the human family, built in solidarity on the basis of the fundamental values of justice and peace" (nos. 53–54). On this account, artificial barriers separating peoples lose their primacy, or at least their importance, and must be seriously modified. Globalization should make it clear today how boundaries of any sort, including national ones, are not a protection against the consequences of underdevelopment and development devoid of ethics. Marginalization of peoples or the destruction of the environment in one area of the world affects the meaning of authentic development everywhere. The overarching threat of terrorism, the HIV and AIDS pandemic, trafficking in harmful drugs, and the phenomenon of migration for political, economic and other reasons that the world is experiencing are just a few indications of this fact. For true development, the reality that the world is interdependent must be taken seriously.

Solidarity does not do away with, but in fact presupposes respect for personal integrity, national identity, cultural plurality, subsidiarity and dialogue. Just as "the relation between individual and community is a relation between one totality and another," Pope Benedict XVI correctly argues, "so too the unity of the human family does not submerge the identities of individuals, peoples and cultures, but makes them more transparent to each other and links them more closely in their legitimate diversity." Even the desirable establishment of some form of "world political authority" to better regulate globalization and its effects cannot afford to obscure the identity upon which the dignity of individuals, peoples and cultures is built (nos. 54, 67).

For development in Africa this implies several broad things. One is that, despite the globalization movement and, in fact, perhaps because of it, there is need for African countries to rethink the current dominant development theories and approaches. In the majority of cases, they must devise their own standards, methods and processes of development based on their physical and cultural realities, their own needs as they see them and directed toward their own goals. Although in the spirit of universal cross-fertilization they must be ready to learn from others' experiences, their own experience will be their road map.

The meaning and goal of African development must not necessarily be to imitate or catch up with the West, but to make sure that African people enjoy the good life. The basic essentials of the good life still pertain to the acquisition of sufficient food, clothing and shelter, and the availability of education and health facilities. But it is not possible to reach these goals without sound systems of governance in the continent, systems that uphold the rights and dignity of the person and promote justice and equity. This is another condition for development in Africa.

A third crucial element in African development is African imagination, the importance of initiating constructive thoughts and implementing them. Pope Benedict XVI brings this out forcefully to African thought and processes of development. Africans themselves must imagine ways of promoting social, economic, and cultural rights as well as civil and political rights of the continent's peoples. These are the essential factors called for if true development in Africa in the sense that Pope Benedict XVI's *Caritas in Veritate* speaks of is to happen.

Conclusion

No Turning Back the Clock

ALTHOUGH IN THE LAST fifty years or so since the end of the Council there have been attempts by some people at all levels of the Church to rein in a number of the major theological and pastoral developments it unleashed, Msgr. Bergoglio as Archbishop of Buenos Aires (later to become Pope Francis) insisted to his priests that the Council was "a great work of the Holy Spirit" and that on that issue "there could be no 'turning back the clock.'"[1] In the spirit of its convener, Pope John XXIII, the Council has sought to humanize the Church. Pope John XXIII himself personified the sort of appearance he wished the Church to have: a truly human face. "He smiled, told jokes, was spontaneous in manner and unconcernedly fat. He openly expressed his love for his family." In the mid-twentieth century, "for many Catholics he seemed to be a living image of what they believed or hoped the Church to be, as he described it himself in his opening address to the Council: 'benign, patient, full of mercy and goodness.'"[2]

Pope John XXIII intended the outward appearance of the Church to be truly the expression of its inner being, its nature: a Church that cares, that is both truly interested in the welfare of and works for the wellbeing of the poor; a Church whose goal for the world is reconciliation and peace. It is why, prior to convening the Council and in the midst of great international tension, he had written two encyclicals to this effect—*Mater et Magistra* (1961) on the role of the Church in the process of social development and *Pacem in Terris*

---

1. Vallely, *Pope Francis: Untying the Knots*, 11.
2. O'Malley, *What Happened at Vatican II*, 105.

(1963) on the true path towards peace among nations in the world. Both of these letters marked a change in the Church's stance: from distancing itself from the world and world affairs to insertion in the world to transform it in the manner of salt or yeast.

Following the Council, Pope John XXIII's successors in the papacy have each in his own way represented and promoted this noble, human character of the Church. In this respect, Pope John Paul I was remarkable. During his short pontificate of only thirty-three days, he managed to capture the attention, admiration, and love of the world. Like Pope John XXIII, his immediate predecessor, he too made the papacy look "human" again by his simplicity after centuries of enigmatic symbolism and language surrounding it. For example, he publicly admitted that he had been embarrassed when Pope Paul VI appointed him Patriarch of Venice, a sign of his deep humility. Moreover, on becoming Pope, he discarded the use of the customary royal "We" in his speeches in preference for the common first person singular. Likewise, he was reluctant to use the *sedia gestatoria,* the portable papal chair and preferred to walk. He set a precedent for others on this: no other Pope used the portable throne after him. Furthermore, Pope John Paul I "was the first Pope to choose an 'investiture' [simple installation ceremony] to commence his papacy rather than the traditional Papal Coronation" In his communications, he used modest day-to-day language of the people.[3] Describing himself he said characteristically, "The Pope is a man who laughs, cries, sleeps peacefully, and has friends like everybody else. A normal person."[4]

We mention these facts because, once again, they marked a radical break from the traditional practice of the papacy whose emphasis for almost 1000 years had not been on simplicity and expression of humility and service but on ostentatious power and authority. In different ways, Pope John Paul II (1978–2005) and Pope Benedict XVI (2005–13) continued to personify these changes, signified especially by their travels to different parts of the world in the spirit of pastoral affection and service. But it is Pope Francis who has overwhelmingly sealed the transition by the example of his words, actions, and life.

The selection of his papal name was full of significance for his program of life as leader of what he intended to be a simple, open, and human Church. He wanted his new name to define the entire direction of his papacy. He explains the circumstances of the choice of the name in this way:

> During the election, I was seated next to the Archbishop Emeritus of Sao Paulo and Prefect Emeritus of the Congregation for the

---

3. Pope John Paul I." In The Wikipedia encyclopedia, accessed November 14, 2016. https://en.wikipedia.org/wiki/Pope_John_Paul_I.

4. Pique, *Pope Francis,* 305

Clergy, Cardinal Claudio Hummes: a good friend, a good friend! When things were looking dangerous, he encouraged me. And when the votes reached two-thirds, there was the usual applause, because the Pope had been elected. And he gave me a hug and a kiss, and said: "Don't forget the poor!" And those words came to me: the poor, the poor. Then, right away, thinking of the poor, I thought of Francis of Assisi. Then I thought of all the wars, as the votes were still being counted, till the end. Francis is also the man of peace. That is how the name came into my heart: Francis of Assisi.[5]

Echoes of Pope John XXIII and the Council's program are unmistakable here. By taking this name, Pope Francis intended to make it known that he eschewed unnecessary ostentation in the office of papacy and in the Church at large. And, like Pope John Paul I, he started to demonstrate this immediately. As Paul Vallely reports, he declined to wear "the traditional ceremonial elbow-length red velvet cape, trimmed with ermine—the mozzetta." There are other traditional papal paraphernalia that he equally instantly declined. They included a golden pectoral cross, luxurious papal cufflinks, and the customary red shoes. When offered the latter, he looked down at the old "dilapidated" black ones he had worn throughout the conclave and remarked that they were fine for him.[6] He also refused to live in the spacious papal apartments, the Apostolic Palace in the Vatican, where Popes have lived since 1903. He chose instead to reside at the simpler Domus Sanctae Marthae, a guesthouse for clergy near St. Peter's Basilica.

As already mentioned, all of these symbolic gestures had deep implications for the papacy and the Church. They were reversing years of history in Church attitude, from pomp and circumstance to service and humility. It must be underlined again, however, that although dramatized very visibly by Pope Francis, they were nonetheless not a sudden inspiration to him at his election. Although ordained priest four years after the Council (1969) and consecrated bishop much later (1992), by his training as a member of the Society of Jesus and as Provincial Superior of the Society in Argentina (1973–79) he must have been familiar with the contents and the spirit of Vatican II. As we have been trying to show throughout this book, the roots for a different face of the Church that he is trying to foster conspicuously lie there.

During the Council deliberations, there was tension between two major opposing perspectives about the shape of the Church. The emotional and intellectual situation that prevailed consisted of those who wanted to retain the status quo established by Trent and Vatican I on the one hand, and those,

---

5. Vallely, *Pope Francis*, 161.
6. Vallely, *Pope Francis*, 162–63. See also Pique, *Pope Francis*, 19–36, 167–80.

on the other, like Pope John XXIII were in favor of *aggiornamento*, or change in the structure and behavior of the Church: from hierarchical to horizontal, from didactic to dialogical, and from imperial to more collegial manner of Church. The documents of the Council and what has taken place in the Church since shows that the latter position finally had the upper hand. But conversion was neither instant nor easy; after a millennium of build-up to the former it could not have been. There were of course strong remnants of resistance against change after the Council, some of which have survived to the present, with a glaring example being that of Archbishop Marcel Lefebvre and his Priestly Society of St. Pius X.

Pope Francis realizes this tension in his struggle to impress upon the Church the necessity of change since his election. Having experienced some kind of conversion in his own life,[7] reminiscent to that of such figures in the history of Christianity as Paul of Tarsus, Augustine of Hippo and, more recently, Archbishop Oscar Romero of San Salvador, El Salvador, he is tenacious and hope-filled in what he is doing. He is building upon the revolutionary aspects of the Council and his predecessors since then to shape a new way of being Church in its spirituality and structures. What the prospects are in some dimensions of the Church in Africa is what we have been trying to gauge. What has happened there and what is to be expected? In conclusion, let us briefly identify and assess a few key points.

An important area where the Council's spirit of *aggiornamento* has influenced the Church in Africa is structural. The pre-conciliar absolutist and centralizing attitude of the Church by many African bishops is still to be observed in various dioceses across the continent and is guarded jealously there. In this view the bishop and the clergy are still the main players in the particular (diocesan) Church. The joke that lay people are there to "pay, pray, and obey" is sadly still too real in these places. Despite the assertion that the Church is the "people of God," it is in actual fact seen to be constituted by the clergy. During the First African Synod the bishops described the Church as "family of God," but in these dioceses the structure of this family is still to be defined to align itself with the changed ecclesiology of the Council.

But it must be said that even in these places, there is an experience of change, seen most evidently in the growth and development of Small Christian Communities (SCCs) spreading across the continent. Where they have been established and are flourishing, "SCCs are an important pastoral strategy and even a new way of being a communitarian Church"[8] rather than a strictly hierarchical one. SCCs reflect a new way of being Church in Africa, a "restruc-

---

7. Pique, *Pope Francis*, 61–82.
8. Healey and Hinton, *Small Christian Communities Today*, 97.

turing process," whereby the Church arises from and is primarily based on the faith of the faithful, the *sensus fidei fidelium*. In this paradigm, ministries and pastoral action, although coordinated by the clergy and hierarchy for the sake of unity and order, begin and are galvanized here. It is at this level, where people are intimately connected, know one another, and help one another out, that the human face of the Church reveals itself.

At the level of SCCs too, ministries arise motivated by real needs of the people. Because of this, lay formation is needed and has been undertaken in various local Churches. An example is the establishment of pastoral and catechetical centers for the purpose. The responsibility for innovation is therefore not concentrated exclusively in the hands of the ordained ministry as was the case in the past, but is spread out among the faithful as the Spirit of God prompts, in line with a new emphasis on an ecclesiology of communion that the Council called for. The movement is in accord with Pope Francis's insistence on the necessity of "change of attitude" which involves the fight against "temptations" like "the ideologization of the Gospel message, the functionalism 'that reduces the reality of the Church to the structure of an NGO [a nongovernmental, nonprofit organization], where what is of value is the ascertainable result and statistics and clericalism." Of course, the bishop as leader must lead, but Pope Francis insists that leading in the new ecclesiology "is not the same thing as giving orders."[9]

It is necessary to have a system in place to push this insight forward in Africa. What is lagging behind seems to be the insertion of this new ecclesiological vision in the training of the clergy in many seminaries. Seminary formation in Africa is still deeply Tridentine, steeped in the mentality of leadership as issuing directives rather than dialogue and consensus. The indigenous African palaver paradigm of governance should be of great help here. Unfortunately, priestly formation does not emphasize looking honestly and critically into the structures of the Church and identifying and trying to correct "structural sins" embedded there on account of human weakness which, in 2000, Pope John Paul II summarized in six categories as offences "in the service of truth"; those that have harmed Church unity; anti-Semitism; offenses against cultural and religious rights; against the dignity of women; against human rights.[10] Without doubt, Pope Francis would endorse this confession.[11]

---

9. Pique, *Pope Francis*, 276.

10. See Baum, *Amazing Church*, 79.

11. See Hamel, Gary and Tennant, "The 5 Requirements of a Truly Innovative Company" accessed May 12, 2016. https://hbr.org/2015/04/the-5-requirements-of-a-truly-innovative-company

New political, economic, and social awareness taking place in Africa in particular should make seminary formation to take this responsibility more seriously. To construct a new, engaged Church, instruction included in seminary curricula must take into account the importance of the social teaching of the Church, the question of reconciliation and peace, ecumenism and interreligious dialogue, and African Religion. On the latter, Pope John Paul II in *Ecclesia in Africa* (no. 67) called for a new attitude from the Church. Instead of ridicule and the dismissive approach predominant previously, he urged that "The adherents of African traditional religion should . . . be treated with great respect and esteem, and all inaccurate and disrespectful language should be avoided." In terms of formation, he emphasized that "suitable courses in African traditional religion should be given in houses of formation for priests and religious." More than fifty years after the Council, there has not been enough mutually respectful engagement between Christianity and African Religion. This is perhaps the biggest hindrance against the Church's *aggiornamento* in Africa. Reluctance to look at African Religion with the respect it deserves amounts, in the expression of John Paul II, to a "sin" against African culture and the African person. Moreover, it prevents the message of Christ from sending deep roots into the African soil.

There are many setbacks against the spirit of Vatican II blossoming fully in the Church in Africa. This is to be expected; it has been part and parcel of the History of Salvation. Yet, faith in the divine presence amongst us, the Church in Africa, in spite of our unfaithfulness, and hope in the work of the Spirit of God producing works of charity must impel us forward on this pilgrim way. As Pope Francis encourages every faithful in *Evangelii Gaudium* (no. 121), his words have particular relevance to Africa:

> Of course, all of us are called to mature in our work as evangelizers. We want to have better training, a deepening love and a clearer witness to the Gospel. In this sense, we ought to let others be constantly evangelizing us. But this does not mean that we should postpone the evangelizing mission; rather, each of us should find ways to communicate Jesus wherever we are. All of us are called to offer others an explicit witness to the saving love of the Lord, who despite our imperfections offers us his closeness, his word and his strength, and gives meaning to our lives. In your heart you know that it is not the same to live without him; what you have come to realize, what has helped you to live and given you hope, is what you also need to communicate to others. Our falling short of perfection should be no excuse; on the contrary, mission is a constant stimulus not to remain mired in mediocrity but to continue growing. The witness of faith that each Christian is called to offer leads

us to say with Saint Paul: "Not that I have already obtained this, or am already perfect; but I press on to make it my own, because Christ Jesus has made me his own" (Phil 3:12–13).[1]

Select Bibliography

Abbott, Walter M., and Joseph Gallagher. *The Documents of Vatican II.* New York: Guild, 1966.
Agbasiere, Joseph T., and Boniface K. Zabajungu, eds. *Church Contribution to Integral Development.* Eldoret, Kenya: AMECEA Gaba, 1989.
"Aggiornamento." In The Wikipedia encyclopedia. Accessed September 12, 2011. https://en.wikipedia.org/wiki/Aggiornamento#cite_note-3.
Allport, G. Willard. *The Individual and His Religion.* New York: Macmillan, 1962.
Altaner, Berthold. *Patrology.* Freiburg: Herder and Herder, 1960.
Anderson, David. *Histories of the Hanged: Britain's Dirty War and the End of Empire.* London: Phoenix, 2005.
Anderson, David M., and Douglas H. Johnson, eds. *Revealing Prophets: Prophecy in Eastern African History.* London: Currey, 1995.
Appiah-Kubi, Kofi, and Sergio Torres, eds. *African Theology en Route: Papers from the Pan-African Conference of Third World Theologians, December 17-23, 1977, Accra, Ghana.* Maryknoll, NY: Orbis, 1979.
Avila, Charles. *Ownership: Early Christian Teaching.* Maryknoll, NY: Orbis, 1983.
Balasuriya, Tissa. "A Missing Dimension in Papal Encyclical." *SEDOS Bulletin* 41:1/10 (2009) 239–44.
Barrett, David B. *Schism and Renewal in Africa: An Analysis of Six Thousand Contemporary Religious Movements.* London: Oxford University Press, 1968.
Barrett, David B. *African Initiatives in Religion: 21 Studies from Eastern and Central Africa.* Nairobi, Kenya: East African, 1971.
Basler, Roy P. *The Collected Works of Abraham Lincoln, Vol. III.* New Brunswick, NJ: Rutgers University Press, 1953.
Baum, Gregory. *Amazing Church: A Catholic Theologian Remembers a Half-Century of Change.* Maryknoll, NY: Orbis, 2005.
Baur, John. *2000 Years of Christianity in Africa: An African Church History.* Nairobi, Kenya: Paulines Publications Africa, 1994.

SELECT BIBLIOGRAPHY

Benedict XVI. *Africae Munus*. Encyclical Letter. Vatican Website. November 19, 2011. http://www.vatican.va/holy_father/benedict_xvi/apost_exhortations/documents/hf_ben-xvi_exh_20111119_africae-munus_en.html.

———. *Caritas in Veritate*. Encyclical Letter. Vatican Website. June 29, 2009. http://w2.vatican.va/content/benedict-xvi/en/encyclicals/documents/hf_ben-xvi_enc_20090629_caritas-in-veritate.html.

———. '*Motu Proprio Data*' *Porta Fidei*. Encyclical Letter. Vatican Website. October 11, 2011. http://w2.vatican.va/content/benedict-xvi/en/motu_proprio/documents/hf_ben-xvi_motu-proprio_20111011_porta-fidei.html, 9.

———. *Porta Fidei*. Encyclical Letter. Vatican Website. October 11, 2011. http://www.annusfidei.va/content/novaevangelizatio/en/magistero/benedetto-xvi/lettera-apostolica—porta-fidei-.html.

Berkley, Bill. *The Graves Are Not Yet Full: Race, Tribe and Power in the Heart of Africa*. New York: Basic, 2001.

Boff, Leonardo. *Fundamentalism, Terrorism and the Future of Humanity*. London: SPCK, 2006.

Bosch, David. *Transforming Mission: Paradigm Shifts in Theology of Mission*. Maryknoll, NY: Orbis, 1991.

Brady, Bernard V. *Essential Catholic Social Thought*. Maryknoll, NY: Orbis, 2008.

Brendon, Piers. *The Decline and Fall of the British Empire 1781–1997*. London: Vintage, 2007.

Brown, I. Corinne. *Understanding Other Cultures*. Englewood Cliffs, NJ: Prentice Hall, 1963.

Catholic Culture Organization. "Opening Address to the Council by Pope John XXIII." catholicculture.org. Accessed September 12, 2011. https://www.catholicculture.org/culture/library/view.cfm?recnum=3233.

Clayton, Anthony. *The Killing Fields of Kenya 1952–1960: British Military Operation against the Mau Mau*. Nairobi, Kenya: Transafrica, 2006.

Cobb, John. *Beyond Dialogue: Toward a Mutual Transformation of Buddhism and Christianity*. Philadelphia: Fortress, 1982.

Collins, Chuck, and Mary Wright. *The Moral Measure of the Economy*. Maryknoll, NY: Orbis, 2007.

Collins, Raymond F. *Models of Theological Reflection*. Lanham, MD: University of America Press, 1984.

Cort, John C. *Christian Socialism: An Informal History*. Maryknoll, NY: Orbis, 1988.

Coward, Harold, "Religious Pluralism and the Future of Religions." In *Religious Pluralism and Truth: Essays in Cross-Cultural Philosophy of Religion*, edited Thomas Dean, 45–86. Albany, NY: State University of New York, 1995.

De Craemer, Willy. *The Jamaa and the Church: A Bantu Catholic Movement in Zaire*. Oxford: Clarendon, 1977.

Dellaire, Romeo. *Shake Hands with the Devil: The Failure of Humanity in Rwanda*. London: Arrow, 2002.

Elkins, Caroline. *Britain's Gulag: The Brutal End of Empire in Kenya*. London: Pimlico, 2005.

Ellis, Stephen, and Gerrie ter Haar. *Worlds of Power: Religious Thought and Political Practice in Africa*. New York: Oxford University Press, 2004.

Fabella, Virginia, and R. S. Sugirtharajah, eds. *Dictionary of Third World Theologies*. Maryknoll, NY: Orbis, 2000.

Fitzmyer, Joseph A. "The Letter to the Romans." In *The New Jerome Biblical Commentary*, 830–68. London: Chapman, 1989.
Follo, Francesco. *Inculturation and Interculturality in John Paul II and Benedict XVI.* Accessed September 12, 2011. http://www.oasiscenter.eu/en/node/5610.
Forum on Religion and Ecology at Yale. "World Council of Churches (WCC) Justice, Peace, and Creation (JPC)." Accessed September 12, 2011. http://fore.yale.edu/religion/christianity/projects/wcc_jpc/.
Freire, Paulo. *Pedagogy of the Oppressed.* New York: Bloomsbury Academic, 1970.
Gallagher, M. Paul. *Clashing Symbols: An Introduction to Faith & Culture.* New York: Paulist, 1998.
Gifford, Paul. *African Christianity: Its Public Role.* London: Hurst, 2001.
Goodreads Incorporation. "Basil the Great." Accessed September 12, 2011. http://www.goodreads.com/quotes/672732-the-bread-which-you-hold-back-belongs-to-the-hungry.
Hamel, Gary, and Nancy Tennant. "The 5 Requirements of a Truly Innovative Company." Accessed September 12, 2011. https://hbr.org/2015/04/the-5-requirements-of-a-truly-innovative-company.
Hastings, Adrian. *Church and Mission in Modern Africa.* London: Burns and Oates, 1967.
———. *A History of African Christianity 1950–1975.* Cambridge: Cambridge University Press, 1979.
Hastings, Adrian et al. *The Arusha Declaration and Christian Socialism.* Dar es Salaam, Tanzania: Tanzania House, 1969.
Healey, Joseph G., and Jeanne Hinton, eds. *Small Christian Communities Today: Capturing the New Moment,* Maryknoll, NY: Orbis, 2005.
Hellwig, Monika K. *What Are the Theologians Saying Now? A Retrospective on Several Decades.* Westminster, MD: Christian Classics, 1992.
Helm, Thomas E. *The Christian Religion: An Introduction.* Upper Saddle River, NJ: Prentice Hall, 1991.
Hick, John. *God Has Many Names.* London: Macmillan, 1980.
Hines, Mary E. "North American 'Impulses' Following Vatican II." *Concilium* 3 (2012) 103–9.
Hyers, Conrad. "Rethinking the Doctrine of Double-Truth: Ambiguity, Relativity and Universality." In *Religious Pluralism and Truth: Essays in Cross-Cultural Philosophy of Religion,* edited by Thomas Dean, 171–88. Albany, NY: State University of New York Press, 1995.
Isichei, Elizabeth. *A History of Christianity in Africa: From Antiquity to the Present.* Grand Rapids: Eerdmans, 1995.
John Paul II. *Centesimus Annus.* Encyclical Letter. Vatican Website. May 1, 1991. http://www.vatican.va/holy_father/john_paul_ii/encyclicals/documents/hf_jp-ii_enc_01051991_centesimus-annus_en.html.
———. *Ecclesia in Africa.* Encyclical Letter. Vatican Website. September 14, 1995. http://www.vatican.va/holy_father/john_paul_ii/apost_exhortations/documents/hf_jp-ii_exh_14091995_ecclesia-in-africa_en.html.
———. *Laborem Exercens.* Encyclical Letter. Vatican Website. September 14, 1981. http://w2.vatican.va/content/john-paul-ii/en/encyclicals/documents/hf_jp-ii_enc_14091981_laborem-exercens.html

SELECT BIBLIOGRAPHY

———. *Redemptor Hominis*. Encyclical Letter. Vatican Website. March 4, 1979. http://www.vatican.va/holy_father/john_paul_ii/encyclicals/documents/hf_jp-ii_enc_04031979_redemptor-hominis_en.html.

———. *Redemptoris Missio*. Encyclical Letter. Vatican Website. December 7, 1987. http://www.vatican.va/holy_father/john_paul_ii/encyclicals/documents/hf_jp-ii_enc_07121990_redemptoris-missio_en.html.

———. *Solicitudo Rei Socialis*. Encyclical Letter. Vatican Website. December 30, 1987. http://www.vatican.va/holy_father/john_paul_ii/encyclicals/documents/hf_jp-ii_enc_30121987_sollicitudo-rei-socialis_en.html.

———. *Tertio Millenio Adveniente*. Encyclical Letter. Vatican Website. November 10, 1994. http://www.vatican.va/holy_father/john_paul_ii/apost_letters/documents/hf_jp-ii_apl_10111994_tertio-millennio-adveniente_en.html.

———. *Ut Unum Sint*. Encyclical Letter. Vatican Website. May 25, 1995. http://www.vatican.va/holy_father/john_paul_ii/encyclicals/documents/hf_jp-ii_enc_25051995_ut-unum-sint_en.html.

———. *Veritatis Splendor*. Encyclical Letter. Vatican Website. August 6, 1993. http://www.vatican.va/holy_father/john_paul_ii/encyclicals/documents/hf_jp-ii_enc_06081993_veritatis-splendor_en.html.

John XXIII. *Mater et Magistra*. Encyclical Letter. Vatican Website. May 15, 1961. http://w2.vatican.va/content/john-xxiii/en/encyclicals/documents/hf_j-xxiii_enc_15051961_mater.html.

———. *Pacem in Terris*. Encyclical Letter. Vatican Website. April 11, 1963. http://w2.vatican.va/content/john-xxiii/en/encyclicals/documents/hf_j-xxiii_enc_11041963_pacem.html.

Kasper, Walter. "The Continuing Challenge of the Second Vatican Council: The Hermeneutics of the Conciliar Statements." In *Theology and Church*, 166–76. New York: Crossroad, 1989.

Keim, C. *Mistaking Africa: Curiosities and Inventions of the American Mind*. Boulder, CO: Westview, 2000.

Knitter, Paul. *No Other Name? A Critical Survey of Christian Attitudes toward the World Religions*. Maryknoll, NY: Orbis, 1984.

Küng, Hans. *Global Responsibility: In Search for a New World Ethic*. New York: Crossroads, 1991.

Lugard, Frederick D. *The Dual Mandate in British Tropical Africa*. Edinburgh: Blackwood, 1922.

"La Santa Sede." Synodus Episcoporum: Ii Coetus Specialis Pro Africa. Accessed September 12, 2011. http://portal.unesco.org/culture/en/files/12762/11295421661mexico_en.pdf/mexico_en.pdf.

———. Synodus Episcoporum: Ii Coetus Specialis Pro Africa. Accessed September 12, 2011. http://www.vatican.va/roman_curia/synod/documents/rc_synod_doc_20091023_elenco-prop-finali_en.html.

Lochhead, David M. *The Dialogical Imperative: A Christian Reflection on Interfaith Encounter*. Maryknoll, NY: Orbis, 1988.

Magesa, Laurenti. *African Religion in the Dialogue Debate: From Intolerance to Coexistence*. Vienna: LIT Verlag, 2010.

———. *Rethinking Mission: Evangelization in Africa in a New Era*. Eldoret, Kenya: AMECEA Gaba, 2006.

SELECT BIBLIOGRAPHY

Manwelo, Paulin. "The Politics of Identity in Africa: Diversity and Inclusion." In *Ethnicity, Conflict, and the Future of African States*, edited by Aquiline Tarimo and Paulin Manwelo, 107–18. Nairobi:, Kenya Paulines Publications Africa, 2009.

Massaro, Thomas. "Christian Socialism." In *The Cambridge Dictionary of Christianity*, edited by Daniel Patte, 212–13. Cambridge: Cambridge University Press, 2010.

Maxwell, J. Francis. *Slavery and the Catholic Church: The History of Catholic Teaching Concerning the Moral Legitimacy of the Institution of Slavery*. Chichester, UK: Rose, 1975.

Mejia, Rodrigo, ed. *The Conscience of Society*. Nairobi, Kenya: Paulines Publications Africa, 1995.

———. "Message to the People of God of the Second Special Assembly for Africa of the Synod of Bishops." In Assembly for Africa of the Synod of Bishops, accessed September 12, 2011. http://www.vatican.va/roman_curia/synod/documents/rc_synod_doc_20091023_message-synod_en.html.

Mugambi, Jesse N. K., and Frank K. Pelkmann, eds. *Church-State Relations: A Challenge for African Christianity*. Nairobi, Kenya: Acton, 2004.

Nasimiyu-Wasike, A., and Douglas W. Waruta. "Introduction." In *Mission in African Christianity: Critical Essays in Missiology*, edited by A. Nasimiyu-Wasike and Douglas W. Waruta, 1–9. Nairobi, Kenya: Uzima, 1993.

Nazir-Ali, Michael. *Mission and Dialogue: Proclaiming the Gospel Afresh in Every Age*. London: SPCK, 1995.

Neill, Stephen. *Christian Faith and Other Faiths: The Christian Dialogue with Other Religions*. London: Oxford University Press, 1961.

Neuner, Josef, and Jacques Dupuis. *The Christian Faith*. New York: Alba House, 1986.

Nyerere, Julius K. *Freedom and Development/Uhuru na Maendeleo*. Dar es Salaam, Tanzania: Oxford University Press, 1973.

———. *Freedom and Socialism/Uhuru na Ujamaa: A Selection from Writings and Speeches*. Dar es Salaam, Tanzania: Oxford University Press, 1968.

O'Brien, David, and T. Shannon, eds. *Renewing the Earth: Catholic Documents on Peace, Justice and Liberation*. Garden City, NY: Image, 1977.

O'Malley, John W. *What Happened at Vatican II*. Cambridge: Belknap (Harvard University Press), 2008.

Orobator, Agbonkhianmeghe E. "Church, State, and Catholic Ethics: The Kenyan Dilemma." *Theological Studies* 70, no. 1 (2009) 182–85.

———. *From Crisis to Kairos: The Mission of the Church in Time of HIV/AIDS, Refugees and Poverty*. Nairobi, Kenya: Paulines, 2005.

———, ed. *Reconciliation, Justice, and Peace: The Second African Synod*. Maryknoll, NY: Orbis, 2011.

Paul VI. *Africae Terrarum*. Encyclical Letter. Vatican Website. October 29, 1967. https://w2.vatican.va/content/paul-vi/it/apost_letters/documents/hf_p-vi_apl_19671029_africae-terrarum.html.

———. *Evangelii Nuntiandi*. Encyclical Letter. Vatican Website. December 8, 1975. http://w2.vatican.va/content/paul-vi/en/apost_exhortations/documents/hf_p-vi_exh_19751208_evangelii-nuntiandi.html.

Pastoral Institute of Eastern Africa. *Development Projects: Examples of Church Involvement in Eastern Africa*. Kampala, Uganda: Gaba, 1971.

Paris, Peter J. *Religion and Poverty: Pan-African Perspectives*. Durham, NC: Duke University Press, 2009.

SELECT BIBLIOGRAPHY

Phan, Peter C. *Being Religious Interreligiously: Asian Perspectives on Interfaith Dialogue*. Maryknoll, NY: Orbis, 2004.

———. *Social Thought: Message of the Church Fathers*. Wilmington, DE: Glazier, 1984.

Pius XI. *Quadragesimo Anno*. Encyclical Letter. Vatican Website. May 15, 1931. http://w2.vatican.va/content/pius-xi/en/encyclicals/documents/hf_p-xi_enc_19310515_quadragesimo-anno.html.

Pique, Elizabetta. *Pope Francis: Life and Revolution—A Biography of Jorge Bergoglio*. Chicago: Loyola, 2013.

Pontifical Council for Interreligious Dialogue. "Dialogue and Proclamation: Reflections and Orientations on Interreligious Dialogue and Proclamation of the Gospel of Jesus Christ." Accessed September 12, 2011. http://www.shinmeizan.com/images/PDF/DialProc-en.pdf.

"Pope John Paul I." In The Wikipedia encyclopedia. Accessed September 12, 2011. https://en.wikipedia.org/wiki/Pope_John_Paul_I.

"Pope John XXIII Convokes the Second Vatican Council." Accessed September 12, 2011. www.diocesecc.org/pictures/Vatican%20Documents/humanae-salutis.pdf.

Quasten, Johannes. *Patrology. Vol I–III*. Westminster, MD: Christian Classics, 1985.

"Reinhold Niebuhr." In New World Encyclopedia. Accessed September 12, 2011. http://www.newworldencyclopedia.org/entry/Reinhold_Niebuhr.

Rendina, Claudio. *The Popes: Histories and Secrets*. Santa Anna, CA: Seven Locks, 2002.

Sedmak, Clemens. *Doing Local Theology: A Guide for Artisans of a New Humanity*. Maryknoll, NY: Orbis, 2002.

Schreiter, Robert J. *Constructing Local Theologies*. Maryknoll, NY: Orbis, 1986.

———. "Foreword." In *Doing Local Theology: A Guide for Artisans of a New Humanity*, edited by Clemens Sedmak, ix–x. Maryknoll, NY: Orbis, 2002.

———. *The New Catholicity: Theology between the Global and the Local*. Maryknoll, NY: Orbis, 1997.

Shorter, Aylward, and Joseph N. Njiru. *New Religious Movements in Africa*. Nairobi, Kenya: Paulines, 2001.

Spradley, James P., and David W. McCurdy. *Anthropology: The Cultural Perspective*. New York: Wiley & Sons, 1975.

Stinton, Diane B., ed. *African Theology on the Way: Current Conversations*. London: SPCK, 2010.

Tanner, Norman P. *The Councils of the Church: A Short History*. New York: Crossroad, 2001.

Tarimo, Aquiline, and Paulin Manwelo, eds. *African Peacemaking and Governance*. Nairobi, Kenya: Acton, 2007.

———. *Ethnicity, Conflict, and the Future of African States*. Nairobi, Kenya: Paulines, 2009.

Tarimo, Aquiline. *Applied Ethics and Africa's Social Reconstruction*. Nairobi, Kenya: Acton, 2005.

Ter Haar, Gerrie. *How God Became African: African Spirituality and Western Secular Thought*. Philadelphia: Pennsylvania, 2009.

Tienou, Tite. *The Theological Task of the Church in Africa*. Hong Kong: Africa Christian, 1990.

UNESCO. "*Mexico City Declaration on Cultural Policies, World Conference on Cultural Policies Mexico City, 26 July–6 August 1982*. Accessed September 12, 2011. http://

SELECT BIBLIOGRAPHY

portal.unesco.org/culture/en/files/12762/11295421661mexico_en.pdf/mexico_en.pdf.

Valleley, Paul. *Pope Francis: Untying the Knots*. New York: Bloomsbury Continuum, 2013.

Van Bergen, Jan. *Development and Religion in Tanzania*. Madras, India: Christian Literature Society, 1981.

Welbourn, F. B. *East African Christian*. London: Oxford University Press, 1965.

Westerlund, D. *Ujamaa na Dini: A Study of Some Aspects of Society and Religion in Tanzania, 1961–1977*. Stockholm: Almqvist & Wiksell, 1980.

Wijsen, Frans, et al., eds. *The Pastoral Circle Revisited: A Critical Quest for Truth and Transformation*. Nairobi, Kenya: Paulines, 2006.

Wrong, Michela, *It's Our Turn to Eat: The Story of a Kenyan Whistle Blower*. London: Fourth Estate, 2009.

www.ingramcontent.com/pod-product-compliance
Lightning Source LLC
Chambersburg PA
CBHW050819160426
43192CB00010B/1819